DICTIONARY OF DREAMS

DICTIONARY

OF

DREAMS

S. JAFAR MAHMUD

Books For All

Delhi - 110 052

Sales Office:
D. K. Publishers Distributors (P) Ltd.
1, Ansari Road, Darya Ganj,
New Delhi - 110002.
Phone : 3261465, 3278368
Fax : 091-011-3264368

Published by:
Books For All
B-2, Vardhaman Palace,
Nimri Commercial Centre, Ashok Vihar,
Phase-IV, Delhi - 110052
Phone : 7401672

Laser Type Set at:
Swastik Typographics
3/35, Street No. 38, Reghar Pura,
Karol Bagh, New Delhi - 110005
Phone : 5736594
Mobile No. : 9811059540

Printed at :
D. K. Fine Art Press (P) Ltd., Delhi - 110052.

PRINTED IN INDIA

A

ABANDON:

of abandoning: Will live a long life. Abandoning your wife: will be in a trouble. Abandoning your husband: Loss of friends. Abandoning your father: Recovery of lost valuables. Abandoning your mother: Illness. Abandoning your children: Loss of money. Abandoning your relatives: Good times are coming. Abandoning yoursweetheart: Will be plunged into debts. Abandoning your lover: Will be guilty of foolish actions. Abandoning your friends: Expect failure in your affairs. Abandoning your home: Happiness. Abandoning your religion: Poverty. Abandoning your business: Quarrels. Abandoning your position: Change for the better. Abandoning influential people: Will have enjoyment in life. Abandoning ship: Failure in business. Abandoning ship and reaching land: Good financial earnings.

ABDOMEN:

of the abdomen: Great expectations. HAving pains in the abdomen: Favourable affairs. Feeling the naked abdomen: Recovery of money. Amarried person dreaming of the abdomen: Unfaithfulness of one mate. A lover's abdomen: Teachery on the part of one of the lovers. A man seeing his abdomen growing: will have high honors. A woman seeing her abdomen growing: She will become pregnant.

ABDUCT:

Being abducted: Plans will be carried out well. Being carried away be force: Good future ahead. A woman being abducted: Very important and beneficial event to come. A child being abducted: A mystery will be solved.

ABHOR:

of abhoring something: Difficulties in your path. Abhorring someone: Inheritance. Abhorring an article and getting rid of it: Worries are over. Being abhorred by others: Are prone to being selfish.

ABODE:

of own abode: False statements are being made against you. Going into a strange abode: Will venture new undertakings. Being in a strange abode: Affairs are in disorder. Being refused admission to an abode: Be cautious in your plans. Being locked out of an abode: Be meticulous in avoiding needless risk.

ABORTION:

of an abortion: End of your love affairs. Having an abortion: Happiness in the family. Performing an abortion: Troubles ahead. A successful abortion: Will live a long life. Others having an abortion: Lonliness and trouble.

ABOVE:

Something hanging above you: Will receive good news. Something falling near you from above: Will escape money losses. Being hit by something falling from above: Sudden death. Something from above falling on others: Beware of jealous friends.

ABROAD:

Going abroad : A change of work will take place. Being abroad: Unsettled mind and way of thinking. Returning from abroad: Changes in present conditions. Others going abroad: Triumph over enemies. Others being abroad: Will be deceived.

ABSCOND:

Someone absconding with your money: Treachery among those nearby. Absconding with money: Will recovery losses. Relatives absconding: Beware of enemies. Friends absconding: Be circumspect in all your dealings.

ABSENT:

A loved one being absent: Danger in love matters. other people being absent: Will have mastery over many matters. Rejoicing over the absence of a relative: Frivolity. Rejoicing over the absence of a friend: Loss of an enemy. The death of an absent friend: A wedding is being planned.

ABSTAIN:

Refusing a dring: Avoid your rivals. Abstaining completely from drinking: Important events, very beneficial. Relatives abstaining from drinking: Will live a long life. Friends abstaining from drinking: Beware of jealous friends.

ABUNDANCE:

Having overbundance: Must calm your bad temper. Having abundance of money: A mystery will be solved. Relatives having abundance of every thing: Approaching money. Others having abundance: Good results in love matters.

ABUSE:

Being abused: Business affairs will go badly. Abusing another person: Others will take advantage of you. Abusing your children: Success in love affairs. Being abused by friends: Warning of troubles.

ACCEPT:

Being accepted: Will have mastery over many matters. A lover being accepted: Affairs will not prosper. Refusing to be accepted: Family quarrels. Accepting an invitatiton: Expect an inheritance.

ACCIDENT:

Of an accident: A warning to avoid unnecessary travel. Being in an accident: Your life is threatened. An accident at sea: Disappointment in love affairs. An accident in the air: Will have a vigorous mind. An accident in the an automobile. Approaching money.

ACCLAIM:

Acclaiming others: Sorrowful consequences. Receiving acclaim: DEprived of original simplicity. Others showing acclaim: Will be double-crossed by friends. Acclaiming a prominent person: Troubles ahead.

ACCOMPANY:

Accompanying someone: Failure of enemies. Being accompanied: Very important and beneficial events to come. Being accompanied by friends: Change of surroundings. Having musical accompaniment: A mystery will be solved. Accompanying a funeral procession: Poverty. Accompanying a close friend to a cemetery: Riches and fortune. Accompanying unknown person to a cemetery: Will be in need of money.

ACCOST:

Being accosted by a man: will be scorned by others. Being accosted by a woman: Honor. Being accosted by a business person: Profit. Being accosted by a poor person: Will receive money. Being accosted by a friend: Will receive a legacy.

ACCOUNTS:

Adding up accounts: Loss of money by giving credit. Working on accounts and bills: Hard work awaits. Figuring others' accounts: Dignity and distinction. Figuring employer's accounts: Beware of enemies.

ACCUSE:

Being accused: Beware of scandal. Accusing others: Danger and misfortune. Proving innocence when accused: Will overcome difficulties. A righteous accusation: Serious troubles ahead. Being accused by others of committing a crime: Will be leset by doubts. Accusing yourself of wrongdoing: Will have plenty of money. Being accused by a secret service official: Will be in trouble. Being accused by a woman: Approaching business disaster. being accused by a man: Big success.

ACE:

The ace of diamonds: Quarrels. The ace of Clubs: Money. The ace of Hearts: Bad luck. The acc of Spades: Good news. Of an ace pilot: Another person is enjoying what you hoped to win. Being an ace pilot: Will be deceived in love matters.

ACHE:

A woman having a severe ache: Very important and beneficial events to come. A man having an ache: Good and prosperous business. A farmer having an ache: Will have a good harvest. A sailor having an ache: Will have a successful trip. A lover having aches: Suitable time to pursue suit.

ACQUAINTANCE:

of an acquaintance: Good luck. Visiting an acquaintance: Will have enjoyment in life. Making new acquaintances: A change in life will soon come. Quarreling with an acquaintance: Your health will not be good. Others being with your acquaintances: Will have a vigorous mind.

ACQUIT:

Being acquitted by a court: Failure of enemies. Not being acquitted: Big prosperity. Guilty people being acquitted: Will experinece ups and downs. Others being acquitted: Will have prosperous business. Others not being acquitted: Misfortune.

ACTING:

Of acting: Plans will not succeed. Others acting: Will take a short trip. Watching actors acting: Friends will cheat you. Watching an actress acting: Will receive a letter with good news. Watching children acting: Will have pleasant work and good news.

ACTOR OR ACTRESS:

Being introduced to an actress: Will have troubles at home. Being introduced to an actor: Beware of much gossip. Seeing many actors and actresses: Big satisfaction in life. Acomedian actor or actress: Good success in present business. A tragin actor or actress: Unhappiness. Being an actor: Loss of friends. Being an actress: Will have much uneasiness.

ADDRESS:

Writing an address: Be careful of entering risky speculations. Others writing an address: Misfortune in business. Writing a business: Luck and prosperity. Writing address on love letters: Will receive good news.

ADIEU:

Bidding adieu to people: Will have bad health. Others bidding adieu to you: Will take a tedious journey. Bidding adieu to mate: Good times are coming. bidding adieu to children: Approaching money.

ADMINISTRATE:

Of an administrator: Disappointment in affairs. Being summoned by an administrator: Improvement in business. Administrating own business: Will receive an inheritance. Administrating others' affairs: Good business activities.

ADMIRE:

Being admired: A change in life will come soon. Admiring other people: Unhappiness. Being admired by someone you like: Friendship. being admired by children: Will live a long life.

ADOPT:

Adopting someone: Relatives will ask for help. Being adopted: Beware of enemies. Having adopted children: Difficulties in love. Being an adopted person: Financial gains.

ADORE:

Adoring children: big success in all affairs. Adoring your

husband: Happiness and long life. Adoring your wife: Wealth. Adoring your sweetheart: Misfortune in business. Adoring or worshiping an idol: Failure of affairs. Adoring God and praying to him: Contentment and joy.

ADORN:

Being adorned: Difficulties and troubles ahead. Adorning your children's room: Good times are coming. Adorning your home: Changes in circumstances soon to come. Others being adorned: Death of a relative.

ADULTERY:

Committing adultery: Your morals are excellent. Other people committing adultery: Loss of money. Wife committing adultery: Quarrels with neighbors. Husband committing adultery: Will receive an inheritance.

ADVANCE:

Advancing in love affairs: Success in business plans. Advancing to become own boss: Success is certain. Advancing in present position: Beware of jealous friends. Advancing in a law suit: Will lose the case.

ADVANTAGE:

Taking advantage: Improvement in affairs in the future. Other taking advantage of you: Will have small disputes. Taking advantage of others: Consolidation of business affairs soon. Taking advantage of poor people: Will receive good news. Friends taking advantage of you: Will lead a life of ease. People taking advantage to get money: Family prosperity in the future.

ADVENTURE:

Being an adventurer: Will be tormented a great deal. Dreaming of exciting adventures: Big change in your future. Going on an adventure with a man: New interest and surroundings. Going on an adventure with a woman: Someone wi watching you. Participating in adventures: Will be bothered by women screaming.

ADVERSARY:

Of an adversary: Will win against rivals. Fighting with adversary: Doomed for disappointment. Having an adversary partner in business: Financial losses. Having an adversary attorney: Worries will be smoothed away. Being an adversary attorney; A false friend is near.

ADVERSITY:

Having adversity: Prosperity. being persecuted by adversity: Discovery of money. Having adversity in business: Will realize high ambitions. Having adversity in love: Be on guard against spiteful fossip.

ADVERTISE:

Placing an advertisement: Difficulties and disappointment ahead. Reading an advertisement: Realization of plans. Advertising a sale: Loss of money. Receiving a favorable advertisement: Social activities of a happy nature.

ADVICE:

Receiving advice: Beware of false friends. Receiving advice from a priest: Loneliness and troubles. Receiving advice from an attorney: Will be humiliated. Giving advice to others: Friendship of many people. Giving advice to children: Hard work ahead. Giving professional advice: See that affairs are carried out well. Giving financial advice: Will receive a large payment.

ADVOCATE:

Being a counselor: Are considered well to do by others. Becoming an advocate: Will have safety and money. Children being an advocate: Happiness is assured. Hiring an advocate to defend you: Will not have good results. Being introduced to an advocate: Bad news to come.

AFFECTION:

Of affection: Troubles for those near you. Having affection: Dignity and distinction. Not having affection: Will have a long life. Affection between two loved ones: Inheritance. Having the affection of children: Will recieve unexpected money.

AFFILIATION:

Affiliating the soul to God: Big joy. Being affiliated with a party: Beware of enemies. Affiliating someone as a member: Will receive many honors. Affiliating with another person: A change for the better to come.

AFFLICT:

Being afflicted: Success is certain. Husband or wife being afflicted: Rapid success in business. Being in a state of affliction: Happy destiny in view. Being afflicted by others: A change for the better is coming soon.

AFFLUENCE:

Of affluence: Big success in plans. Having affluence of wealth: Loss of business and money. Having affluence of property: Loss of an estate. Others having affluence of property and everything: Avoid rivals.

AFFRONT:

Receiving an affrong: Loss of an inheritance. being affronted by relatives: Death in the family. Being affronted by friends: Troubles ahead before having joy. Afforonting others: Must control passions.

AFLOAT:

Seeing something affoat: Will have troubles caused by others. A small boat affoat: Good business ahead. A big ship affoat: Abundant means. A fish affoat: Will have good earnings. A dead person affoat in the sea or, river: Happy destiny ahead.

AFTERNOON:

A beautiful afternoon: Good times are coming. A cloudy afternoon: Very small profits ahead. A foggy afternoon: Have faith in yourself. A rainy afternoon: Will have good profits in business.

AGE:

To worry of your own age: Approaching illness. Other people age: Will have many very close friends. Partner's age: Are being deceived. Relative's age: Death in the family. Friend's age: Will have a vigorous mind.

AGED PEOPLE:

Of an aged person: Joy without profit. Member of family being aged: Approaching money. Several aged people: Good luck and health. Poor aged people: Difficulties ahead.

AGENT:

An agent soliciting: Will have good earnings. being an agent: Will influence people to do good. Having dealings with and agent: Change of surroundings to come. others who are agents: Be circumspect in all your dealings.

AGONY:

Being in agony: Good sign for business affairs. Husband and wife being in agony: Will have plenty of money. Relatives being in agony: Will have a long life. Children being in agony: Financial gains. Others being in agony: Recovery from an illness.

AGREEMENT:

Of an agreement: Dignity and distinction. Reading an agreement without singing it: Friends will cheat you. signing an agreement: Success of plans. Canceling an agreement: Will have uncertain profits. Not going through with an agreemtn: Hard work awaits. Making an agreement with the devil: Big success for fishermen.

AGRICULTURE:

Of agriculture: Abundance. Being an agriculturist: Prosperity. Making money in agriculture: Success will come through hard work. Having difficulties in agriculture: Arguments caused by vanity. Losing money in agriculture: Will receive news of a marriage. An agriculturist measuring land: Must be very diligent. Being new in the agriculture business: Will have security.

AIR:

Clear air and blue sky: Success. Cold air: Unhappiness in family relations. Hot air: Are doing wrong by causing oppression. Misty air: Are being deceived. Foggy air:

Reconsider present plans for action. Damp air: Misfortune will and optimistic hopes. Calm air: Happiness. Stormy air: Will soon have an illness and be in danger.

AIR GUN:

Of an air gun: Should postpone decisions for a little while. Having an air gun: A change in life will soon come. Buying an air gun: Are being deceived. Receiving an air gun: Will be double-crossed in love. others using an air gun: Enemies are endeavoring to destroy you.

AIRPLANE:

An airplane taking off: Success in your affairs. An airplance landing: Beware of jealous friends. Taking a trip in an airplane: Will soon experience many ups and downs. Being in an airplane with a friend: A change in life will soon come. Being in an airplane with a loved one: Will be guilty of foolish actions. Being in an airplane with family: study plans well and will earn money. Being in an airplane disaster but not killed: Financial gains. Being killed in an airplane accident: Must control passions. Others being killed in an airplane accident: Will have a vigorous mind.

ALARM:

Giving an alarm: Speed your plans to completion. Hearing a fire alarm while asleep: Unexpected bad news ahead. Hearing an alarm when awake: A change in life will soon come. Being frightened by an alarm when sleeping: Troubles ahead.

ALIMONY:

Paying alimony: Will get into serious trouble. Receiving alimony: Will have a good future. Refusing to pay alimony;

Are highly considered by others. Collecting alimony: Will live a long life.

ALIVE:

Being alive: Will be blamed for wrongdoings. Being burned alive: Will do bad financial business. Being drowned alive in water: Will have many worries. Being buried alive: Unhappiness. Being alive at the expense of others: Will be short of money. Children being alive: Happy days ahead.

ALLERGY:

Having an allergy: Will receive good news. Being allergic to fruits: Will be persecuted. Children being allergic to flowers: Will acquire new good freinds. others having allergies: Fortune in present enterprises.

ALLIGATOR:

Of an alligator: Are surrounded by enemies. Several alligators: Be careful in making new speculations. Having alligator shoes: A change for the better will come soon. Having alligator handbag: Will have good earnings.

ALMONDS:

Of almonds: Sorrow for a short time. Buying almonds: Triumph over enemies. Eating almonds: Will live a long life. Almonds having a bitter taste: Present ventures will fail.

ALMOND TREE:

Of an almond tree: Riches. An almond tree in blossom: Will have joy and satisfaction. An almond tree with unripened fruit: Troubles ahead. An almond tree with ripe fruit: Happiness in the home.

ALMS:

Of alms: Sorrow caused by affection for another. Receiving alms: Loss of your home. Giving alms freely: Great happiness. Someone begging alms from you: Misfortune if you refuse to give.

ALPHABET:

Of the alphabet: An absent friend will return. Writing the entire alphabet: Unexpected good news to come. Printing the entire alphabet: Worry will be smoothed away. Counting the foreign alphabet: A mystery will be solved.

ALTERATION:

Alterations being made: Will have good earnings. Making various alterations: Promp engagement. Making alterations to children's clothes: Happiness in the family. Others making alterations for you: Temptations will come to you.

ALTERCATION:

Having a heated dispute: Avoid revals. Having altercation with relatives: Watch neighbors carefully. Having an altercation with a loved one: Happiness in love. Having an altercation with a friend: Pride will be injured. Others having an altercation: Failure of enemies.

AMBULANCE:

Afull ambulance: Realization of all dcsires. An empty ambulance: Loss of a friend. Calling an ambulance for a relative: Will have financial troubles. Calling an ambulance for yourself: Will soon recover from an illness.

AMOROUS:

Being an amorous person: Will be a victim of scandal. Others being amorous toward you: Be careful in love affairs. A man being amorous: Be careful of relationships with others. A woman being amorous: Are demanding too much. Young girls being amorous: Will make a wrong marriage.

AMPUTATE:

Seeing an amputation: Will have a healthy life. A leg being amputated: Loss of a friend. An arm being amputated: Loss of a relative. A hand being amputated: Death of an enemy. A foot being amputated: Death of a friend.

AMULET:

Of an amulet: Beware of jealous friends. Wearing an amulet: Important decision must be made soon. Buying an amulet for protection against evil: Will marry soon. Selling an amulet: Unhappiness. Receiving a gift of an amulet: Will experience the loss of a lover.

AMUSEMENT:

Of a place of amusement: Use your time more wisely. Amusing yourself: Unhappiness. Amusing yourself and family: Will have arguments. Amusing yourself with friends: Loss of money. Amusing yourself with a sweetheart: Will have very high hopes. Others amusing themselves: Will marry a dancer.

ANARCHIST:

Of an anarchist: New interests and surroundings. Several anarchists: Use caution in financial affairs. An anarchist being killed: Will live a long, honest life. Being an anarchist: Loss of freedom.

ANCESTORS:

Of ancestors: Don't trust people who say they are in love. Ancestors who are dead: Happiness. Great grandparents: Small illness to come. Grandparents: Speedy recovery from an illness. other people's ancestors: Fortune is ahead.

ANCHOR:

An anchor on the bow of a ship: Good fortune. An anchor hanging on the side of a ship: luck and prosperity. An anchor being down in the water: Will have disappointments. Raising an anchor from the water: Will have good earnings. Losing an anchor: Financial gains.

ANECDOTE:

Hearing an anecdote: Big social event to come. Telling an anecdote: Important and very beneficial event to come. hearing an anecdote from someone on stage: Doomed for disappointment. Hearing an anecdote from a friend: A mystery will be solved.

ANGEL:

Of an angel: Success in love. Several angels: Will receive an inheritance. A nonsinful person dreaming of an angel: Will receive honors. A sinful person dreaming of an angel: Will have to repent. A healthy person dreaming of an angel: Happiness. An ill person dreaming of an angel: Death. An angel coming into your home: Prosperity. An angel being close to you: Will enjoy peace and well-being.

ANGER:

Being angry: Avoid rivals. Becoming very angry: Will be so upset that you cannot catch your breath. Becoming angry with a loved one: Important events. Becoming angry with a relative: Will benefit through that person. becoming angry with strangers: Will receive unexpected good news. Becoming angry and fighting: Will enjoy good friendships. becoming angry with children: Will get invitation from a prominent person.

ANGLING:

Of anfling: You are wasting your talents. Angling and catching fish: Good news will follow. Angling but not catching fish: Evil will come to you. Angling in the deep sea: Will be alone & annoyed. Angling in a river: Loss of a friend. Angling with nets: Will do business with a smart woman. Telling others of going angling: They will gossip about you. Others going angling: Worry will be smoothed away.

ANIMALS:

Caressing animals: A big fortune is ahead. Feeding animals: Wealth. Beating animals: Expect joy. Beating animals to death: good results in business. Pushing animals away: Will soon be divorced. Animals resting in a stable: Unfortunate in love. Animals resting in a field: Financial gains. Animals on a mountain: Loss of money in business. a dangerous wild animal: Will have adversity. Being pursued by wild animals: Will be offended by a friend. A bull or cow: Will make good investments. A dog: Prosperity. A horse: Important and very beneficial event to come. A horse: Important and very beneficial event to come. A monkey: Social activities of a happy nature. A crocodile: Poverty. A fat animal: abundance buring the year. A skinny animal: Must endure starvation. A tame animal: Are surrounded by enemies. Talking to animals: Will benefit by associating with people of society. Talking to a dog: Pleasant work and good news. Talking to a parrot: You expect too many favors of other people. A parrot talking to you: The parrot's words will come true. Buying animals: Trouble is ahead. Selling animals: Success will be postponed. Other people's animals: A mystery will be solved.

ANKLE:

Of own ankles: A friend is trying to help you secretly. Ankles being injured: Difficulties followed by success later. Breaking an ankle: Death of someone in a foreign country. Other people's ankles: A mystery will be solved. A woman showing her ankles: Realization of her desires. A man dreaming of beautiful ankles: Health an joy. Having big ankles: Fortune and honor. Having very small ankles: Separation from mate in near future. having extraordinarily large ankles: Happiness secured from people abroad. Having beautiful ankles: Will have plenty of money in old age. Having long ankles: Loss of a son. A man's broken ankle bleeding: Will die faraway from loved ones. A Woman dreaming of a man's ankles: Will lose husband and children. Poor people having nice ankles: Big fortune.

Announce: Making a public announcement: Luck and prosperity. Announcing own marriage: Failure of enemies. Announcing a relative's marriage: Immediate recovery. Others announcing their marriage: Discovery of lost valuables. Announcing family affairs: Divorce is in sight. Announcing a death: Danger through a secret. Announcing a birth: Are being deceived. Announcing the arrival of friends: Troubles ahead. others announcing news to you: A change in life will soon come. A happy announcement: Illness and death.

ANNOY:

Being annoyed: Good fortune ahead for all plans. Annoying others: will have good earnings. Annoying a married person: Avoid rivals. Annoying children: Danger through a secret.

ANT:

Ants at work: Good business activity. Having ants in the house: Illness within the family. Ants climbing a tree: Vexations to come. Ants on food: Happiness is assured.

ANTHEM:

Singing a national anthem: Temptation will come to you. Hearing a national anthem: Happiness. Hearing an anthem at an official ceremony: Will receive good news. Hearing an anthem in church: Illness in the family.

ANTIQUES:

Of antiques: Will live a long life. Buying antiques: Inheritance is forseen. Selling antiques: Big loss of money. Taking advantage of an antiquary in a deal: Increased prosperity.

ANVIL:

Of an anvil: Good results through work. Buying an anvil: happiness is assured. Hitting metals on an anvil: Will have a change in present affairs. Other people using an anvil: Good times are ahead.

ANXIETY:

Having anxiety: Will overcome enemies. Having painful anxiety of the mind: Happy days are ahead. Having anxiety over children: Will have good health. Having anxiety over mate: Troubles are ahead.

APARTMENT:

Being in an apartment: Avoid rivals. Owning an apartment: Family quarrels. Being in an apartment alone: Loncliness and disappointment. Being in an apartment with someone else: Good luck in love. Hiding in an apartment: Will receive costly gifts. The apartment of another person: Troubles ahead.

APOLOGY:

Receiving an apology: Happiness in love. Receiving an apology from children: Will overcome enemies. Apologizing to friends: Return of a former friend. Receiving an apology from a friend: Change of companionship

APPAREL:

Of new apparel: Will encounter domestic troubles. Wearing ragged apparel: Inheritance. Being without any apparel: Unexpected money will reach you. Others without any apparel: Favorable time for love. Waring apparel from a show window: Unexpected death of a relative

APPETITE:

Having a big appetite: Loss of relatives. having a small appetite: Ill health ahead. Having an appetite for a big feast: Loss of money. Losing the appetite: Danger through a secret.

APPLAUSE:

Receiving applause: Are prone to vanity. Giving applause: Are unselfish and not envious of others. Applauding a prominent person: Troubles ahead. Others applauding: Treachery by friends.

APPLES:

Having apples: Big earnings and a good life. Eating sweet apples: Good means and a favorable event. Eating sour apples: Will cause troubles for yourself. Eating appleseauce: Change for the better to come.

APPOINTMENT:

Making an appointment: Will do business with untrustworthy person. Missing an appointment: Are prone to insincerity. Changing time of an appointment: Enemies are within the home. Others missing an appointment: False friends are nearby.

APPREHENSION:

Having apprehension: Do thins your own way as in the past. Having apprehension over children: Will escape a present peril. Having apprehension over finances: Family quarrels. Having apprehension over friends: You expect too many favors.

APPROACH:

Being approached by a woman of quality: Will be humiliated. Being approached by a business man: Good results in projects. being approached by an important person: Honor and profit. Being approached by relative: Family arguments. being approached by friends: Dishonor. being approached strangers: Adversity.

APRON:

Of an apron: Happiness. Wearing an apron: Lasting love. A married woman wearing an apron: Will have ups and downs. An unmarried woman wearing an apron: Will soon be engaged. A man wearing an apron: Change for the better. A widow wearing an apron: Will have several good friends. Tearing an apron: Small benefit. Losting an apron: Danger in love affairs. Having lost an apron: Will lose your sweetheart. Tying an apron: Will receive big honors. Untying an apron: Will lose a loved one. A blue apron: Gossip by other women.

ARBITRATION:

Of an arbitration: Loss of money through injustice. Winning an arbitration: Projects will not succeed. Losing an arbitration: Will have future financial benefits. Being an arbitrator: Important and beneficial events to come.

ARCH:

Of an arch: Wealth and advancement. A damaged arch: Must mend ways in life. Passing under an arch: Many will seek favors from you. The arch of a violin: Others will interfere in love affairs.

ARCHER:

Of an archer: Unhappiness in love matters. Being an archer: Unfitted to fill you position. Being a married archer: Danger is nearby. An unmarried archer: Engagement is near.

ARGUE:

Having an argument: Good and long life. Arguing with family: Troubles caused by prying into affairs of others. Arguing with relatives: Will have a strenuous time. Arguing with an attorney: Troublcs ahead. Arguing with other people: An enemy is seeking your ruin.

ARISE:

Arising very early in the morning: Will make plenty of money. Arising with the sun: Big happiness. Arising from bed: Sickness. Arising from the floor: Troubles and affliction. Arising from a chair: Good news. Arising from a couch: Will receive an unexpected letter. Arising with a loved one: Will have disputes.

ARM:

Of own arms: Victory over enemies. Having a nice arm: Will have good friendships. Having arms covered with hairs: Will be very rich. Having big arms: Big joy ahead. Having small arms: Will have plenty of money. Very thin arms: Will soon be rich. Having unusually big arms: Joy and contentment. Having an arm cut off: Loss of a relative. Having pain in the arms: Unlucky results in business. Dirty arms: Big misery ahead. A man having a broken arm: Family quarrels. A woman having a broken arm: Loss of her husband. Having both arms broken: Illness. Having an accident with the arms: Ill heath within family. Right arm being amputated: Death of a male in the family. Left arm being amputated: Death of a female in the family. Breaking an arm: Big peril ahead. Having skin disease on the arms: Will work hard without profit. Having freckles on the arms: Must mend ways in life.

ARMCHAIR:

Of an armchair: Will receive urgent good news. Many armchairs: Honor and dignity. Sitting in an armchair: High consideration by others. Others sitting in armchairs: Unwelcome quest will come to visit.

ARMS:

Of firearms: Rapid success for own hopes. Having a revolver: Discovery of lost valuables. Having a rifle: Another person is enjoying what you hoped to win. Being armed with guns: Postponement of success. Others being armed with guns: Worry will be smoothed away.

ARMY:

Of an army: War within the family. Several armies of different countries: Fortune and joy. The army of own country: Will have small business success. An army fighting: Treason and persecution.

AROUND:

Going around: Will receive good news. Going around with people of poor morals: Will have an operation. Going around with a loved one: Will receive good news. Going around with children: Gossip by neighbors.

ARRANGE:

Arranging things in the house: Desires will not be realized. Arranging family affairs: Hard work will bring fortune. Arranging business: Misfortune. Arranging clothes: Will receive an unexpected visit. Arranging for a trip: Beware of gossip by friends. Others arranging things: Profit.

ARREST:

Being arrested: Will have misery followed by joy. Being arrested: Misfortune is near. Being released from arrest: Unexpected and sudden success. Others being arrested: Will receive an unexpected gift.

ARRIVAL:

Business people arriving: Good earnings. The arrival of a relative: Loss of money. The arrival of many relatives: Loss in business. The arrival of a friend: Will receive a pleasant surprise. The arrival of a mate: Family reunion. The arrival of children: Happiness.

ARROW:

Being hit by an arrow: Misfortune caused by unsuspected person. Throwing an arrow: Unhappiness. Many arrow: Friends are working against you. Having many arrows: Are surrounded by enemies. A broken arrow: Failure in business. Breaking an arrow: Failure in love.

ARSON:

Arson on land: Change for the better. Arson at sea: Successful ventures. Arson committed to others' homes: Dignity. Arson committed in home causing fire with clear flames: Good employment. Arson committed in home causing fire with dark flames: Financial ruin. Arson committed in home causing fire with small flames: Will be fortunate.

ART:

Of works of art: Honor. Buying works of art: Will have to work hard. Selling works of art: Loss of money. Being an art dealer: Diligence will be compensated.

ARTIST:

Of an artist: Success will be yours. Being an artist: Will receive many honors. Having an artist paint your portrait: Treachery of a friend. Posing for a sculptor: You expect too many favors from others. An artist painting portrait of another: Will risk failure to plans.

ASHAMED:

Being ashamed: Fortune in business. Being ashamed of chastity: Will meet a rich person. Being ashamed of actions: Are stricken with a guilty conscience. Being ashamed of children: Listen to advice of friends. A mate being ashamed of the other: Separation will soon take place.

ASHES:

Of ashes: Loss of something through carelessness. Having ashes in own fireplace: Loss of money. Cremated ashes of a relative: Will live a long life. Cremated ashes of a relative being put in a urn: Approaching money.

ASS:

Of an ass: Will not benefit from quarrels. Riding on a donkey: Will fall into disgrace. Having a donkey: Will have a dispute with best friend. Being pulled by a donkey: Good luck in love affairs. An ass running: Will receive bad news. An ass moving very slowly: Plenty of security is forthcoming. Purchasing an ass: Joy within the family. Selling an ass: Big loss in business. Loading an ass: Good buysiness ahead. A loaded ass: Will make money. Sitting on a donkey: Will have plenty of work and fortune. Childredn sitting on a donkey: Happiness. Taking a donkey out of the stable: Business will be dissolved. Hitting a donkey: Will receive unpleasant news. Being kicked by a donkey: Misfortune in love. Putting shoes on a donkey: Will do hard work in the future. Seeing a donkey dead: Will live a long life. Killing a donkey: Will lose all your fortune: The ears of a donkey: Will be confronted with a big scandal. Hearing a donkey bray: Disgrace within the family. A wild donkey: Are not operating business well. Many donkeys: Will be jilted by lover. Donkeys belonging to others: Will have many loyal friends.

ASSAULT:

Being assaulted: Good information will be given to you. Assaulting others: Monetary gain. Children being assaulted: Family quarrels. others being assaulted: Unhappiness in love affairs.

ASTHMA:

Of asthma: Plans will not work out well. Having asthma: Will recover soon by changing residence to another state. Contracting asthma: Financial gains. Others having asthma: Doomed for disappointment.

ASTONISH:

Being astonished: Are in line to receive a cabinet post. Astonishing other people: Big joy ahead. Being astonished by action of others: Riches. A member of the family acting astonishingly: Will receive good news.

ASTROLOGY:

Of astrology: Happiness. A rich person studying astrology: Loss of money. A poor person studying astrology: Death. Studying astrology at night: Important and very beneficial event to come.

ASTRONOMER:

Of an astronomer: Will realize high ambitions. Being an astronomer: Sickness within the family. Being in the company of an astronomer: failure of enemies. Others being with an astronomer: Will have good earnings.

ASYLUM:

Of an asylum: Will live a long healthy life. Being in an asylum: Serious troubles ahead. Avoiding being put in an asylum: Take care of own health. A young girl dreaming of being in an asylum: Will marry soon.

ATHLETE:

Of an athlete: Family quarrels. Being an athlete: Financial problems. Becoming an athlete: Beware of over doing. Being in the company of an athlete: Avoid rivals.

ATMOSPHERE:

Of atmosphere: Prosperity in money matters. A clear atmosphere: Happiness within the family. Cloudy atmosphere: Are with out faithful friends. Rainy atmosphere: Abundant means. Very stormy atmosphere: Will have financial troubles.

ATTACHMENT:

Having an attachment for unpaid taxes: Will have financial embarrassments. Having an attachment for money due: Dissolution of hopes for future. Putting an attachment upon others: Will have ridiculous disputes. Attaching bank accounts: Be careful in business affairs.

ATTACK:

Of an attack: A mystery will be solved. Being attacked injured: Will suffer an insult. Being attacked but not harmed: Will soon have good fortune. Attacking others: Danger is nearby.

ATTEND:

Attending a wedding: Immediate recovery. Attending a funeral: Will have changes for the better. Attending a party: Good times are coming. Attending a dinner party: Accord among friends. Others attending a party: Beware of rivals. Attending to other people's affairs: Temptation will come. Other attending to your affairs: Loss of a friend.

ATTENDANT:

Of an attendant: Dignity and distinction. Having an attendant: Advancement within present position. Dismissing an attendant: Love affairs will be disturbed. others having attendants: Will be cheated by friends.

AUDIENCE:

Of an audience: Will receive high distinction. Having an audience with a prominent person: Will have good earnings. Having an audience with a political person: Good times are coming. Having an audience with a priest: will soon be in trouble. Having an audience with social people: Will have pleasure and distinction.

AUNT:

Of an aunt: Success in money matters. Being an aunt: A successful matri mony is being planned. Husband's aunt: Good times are coming. Wife's aunt: Beware of jealous friends. Visiting with an aunt: Will receive a legacy. Other people's aunts: Shame and sorrow.

AUTHOR:

Of an author: Happiness. Dealing with an author: Good times are coming. Married people dreaming of an author: Fortune within the family. Single people dreaming of an author: Unexpected good news to come. A promoter dreaming of an author: Should handle his business better.

AUTHORITIES:

Of authorities: Troubles ahead. Being called before government authorities: Will receive insults. Seeking help from government authorities: Will incur debts. Being persecuted by government authorities: Advancement within position. Others being before government authorities: Danger through a secret.

AUTOMATIC:

Automatic machines: Will have a change for the better. Acting automatically: Own weaknesses will be discovered. Having automatic power: Good events will come as a surprise. Handling automatic machines: Approaching money.

AUTOMOBILE:

Of an automobile: Hasty news will be sent to you. Owning an automobile: Will receive an important gift. Riding alone in an automobile: new surroundings are anticipated. Riding with family in an automobile: Will be confronted by gossip. riding with lover in an automobiles Must control passions. Riding with sweetheart in an automobile: Own weaknesses will be known. Riding with others in an automobile: be on guard against false news. Having an automobile accident: Approaching money. Escaping from the path of an overturning automobile: Avoid rivals. Riding with friends in an automobile: Will soon discover a secret. Riding with a woman: Scandal will be brought upon your name.

AUTUMN:

Of autumn: Will have a change of surroundings. Autumn in the spring: Unfriendly influences are nearby. Autumn in the summer: Will experience many ups and downs. Autumn in the winter: Good times are coming.

AVALANCHE:

Of an avalanche: Are confronted by insurmountable obstacles. Seeing an avalanche: will soon have good fortune. Being buried under an avalanche of snow: Good profits.

Others being buried under an avalanche: Change of surroundings.

AVOCADO:

Having avocados: Will receive a marriage proposal. Buying avocados: Will be loved by many people. Eating avocados: Will be visited by a loved one. Making a salad with avocados: Good times are coming.

AWAKEN:

Being awakened: Be on guard against coming troubles. Awakening yourself: Will have very good business success. Awakening the family: Failure of enemies. Awakening other people: Favourable events to come.

AX :

Owning an ax: A danger can be averted by own bravery. Swinging an ax: Will receive a business promotion. A rusty or broken ax: Loss of fortune. A man dreaming of an ax: Will have love troubles. A woman dreaming of an ax: Will have a loved person worthy of her. A young woman dreaming of an ax: Will have a wealthy lover.

AXLE:

Of an axle: Recovery from an illness. The axle of a wheel on a car: Will be guided by others. The axle of a wheel on a truck: Will have ill health. The axle on a machine: Abundant means. A broken axle: Beware of enemies.

B

BABY:

A beautiful baby: Will have happiness. A woman dreaming of a baby: Pregnancy. A married, pregnant woman dreaming of a baby: Big success in love. A married woman dreaming of having a baby when not pregnant: Happiness. A single woman dreaming of having a baby: Sorrow. A widow dreaming of having a baby: Avoid rivals. A widow dreaming of expecting a baby: Success in everything. A baby sucking milk from mother's breast: Pleasure in life. A baby sucking milk from a wet nurse: Painful illness. A very smart baby: Will be surrounded by good friends. An ugly baby: Misfortune ahead. Holding a baby on your breast: Will soon have another baby. A baby in swadding clothes: Good hope in love. A baby taking the first steps: Difficulties in business. A woman nursing a baby: Will be deceived by a trusted person. A baby being sick: serious illness within the family. Hearing a baby crying: Disputes in the family. A helpless baby: Disappointments in love. A baby in a bed: Are being watched by one with evil intentions. Other people's babies: Failure of enemies. Many babies: Abundance in your life.

BACHELOR:

Of a bachelor: Beware of deceitful people. Being a bachelor: A change in life will soon come. A young bachelor: Will find a rich widow to mary. An old bachelor: Misfortune in love affairs. Becoming a bachelor after an annulled marriage: Financial gains. A middle-aged man being a bachelor: Big joy in life. An old man being a bachelor: Loss of a friend. A young man being a bachelor: Will marry soon. A bachelor getting married: Will find a rich woman to marry.

BACK:

Of own back: Misfortune in life and will die in misery. Back being broken: Will have ulcers. Back being full of sores: You have many enemies. A woman turning her back on you: Opposition in love. A man turning his back on you: Serious difficulties. A person walking away from you: Jealous people are against you. A person turning around and facing you: Will be spared from illness. A young girl turning her back on you: Wealth. A young man turning his back on a young girl: Loss of money.

BACK DOOR:

Using the back door: Will have good changes in life soon. Letting a lover go out the back door: Will be married soon. Relatives entering the back door: Family arguments. Friends entering the back door: Caution must be used in business ventures. Robbers breaking down the back door: Approaching money.

BADGE:

Of a badge: Are under observation for a promotion. A badge being pinned on you: Big security. Pinning a badge on others: Warning of troubles. Pinning a badge on a policeman: Family reunion. Enemies wearing a badge: Treason and unfaithfulness.

BAG:

Of traveling bags: Abundance. Carrying only one bag:

Will incur plenty of debts. Carrying several bags: Treachery from a friend. Bags being on a wagon: Business will push forward. Bags in a car: Unexpected money will arrive. Other people's Misfortune in love affairs.

BAGGAGE:

Baggage being inside the house: Cancellation of a trip. Baggage being on the street: Belongings will be stolen. Losing your baggage: An inheritance will soon come. Being unable to find baggage: Will be provoked by others. Other people's baggage: Changes in love matters will occur.

BAIL:

Requesting bail: Present condition in life will improve. Furnishing bail: Trouble will arise with an old friend. Not granting bail: Will soon have a change in affairs. Forfeiting bail: Good times are coming.

BAKERY:

Of a bakery: Will be rich. Owing a bakery: Prosperity and success. Being at a bakery: Will have a prosperous year. A baker at work in a bakery: Will receive good news. Being a baker at a bakery: Profits in business ventures.

BAKING:

A married woman dreaming of baking: Unlucky events to come. A single woman dreaming of baking: Loss of friends through bad temper. A widow dreaming of baking: Expect too many favors from others. A man dreaming of baking: Will have plenty of money.

BALCONY:

Standing on a balcony: Will lose present position. Sitting

on a balcony: Will be unable to keep what you now have. Being on a balcony alone: Financial gains. Being on a balcony with a person of opposite sex: Big love. Lovers saying farewell on a balcony: A long separation will follow. Leaving a balcony with a loved one: Big disappointments.

BALD:

Going bald: Serious illness is in sight. Being bald all over the head: Will be loved very much. Being bald in the front of the head: Will be in big trouble. Being bald in the back of the head: Will live in poverty. Being bald on the right side of the head Death of a friend. Being bald on the left side of the head: Death of the relative. A woman going bald: Will have difficulties in love affairs. A baby being bald: Will enjoy love.

BALLET:

A woman dreaming of a ballet: Warning of troubles. A young woman dreaming of a ballet: Infidelity with her lover. A man dreaming of a ballet: Failure in business. A widow dreaming of a ballet: Will soon marry a rich banker. A stage ballet with professional dancers: Will have poor health.

BALLOON:

Of a balloon: Inventive mind will cause disappointment. Being in a balloon: Happiness is assured. Ascending in a balloon:

Will have misfortune during a journey. Decending in a balloon: Will make unfavorable money ventures.

BALLOT:

A ballot box: Present surroundings are not good. Casting a ballot: Will have a change of companionship. Others casting their ballot: Defeat in present affairs. Opening a ballot box: A change for the better to come.

BALM:

Of balm: Are hated by others. Buying balm: Will have a change in environment. Using a soothing balm: True friendship is nearby. Others using balm: Will experience emotional sorrow.

BANANA:

Buying bananas: Prosperity. Eating bananas: Will be imposed upon to fulfill some duty. Selling bananas: Unprofitable business ahead. DEcaying bananas: Will undertake a distasteful affairs. Growing bananas: Will have a small business venture.

BANDIT:

Of a bandit: Prosperity in own affairs. Several bandits: Are in big danger. Being attacked by a bandit: Beware of accidents. Attacking a bandit: Rely upon own vigor and good judgement.

BANK:

Being in a bank: Will receive false promises. Dealing with a bank: Sudden loss of money. Owning a bank: Friends are making fun of you. Borrowing money from a bank: Financial losses ahead. Receiving money from a bank: Bankruptcy is near. Being in a money changer's bank: Will receive unpleasant news.

BAR:

Of a bar: Will be guilty of foolish actions. Having a drink alone in a bar: A false friend is nearby. Drinking with company in a bar: Must control passions. Others drinking in a bar: Are more highly esteemed by friends than realized. Single women drinking in a bar: Financial gains.

BARBER:

Being in a barber shop: Difficulties in business. Going to the barber: Success as a result of applied hard work. Being a barber: Will have big success. Calling a barber to the home: Will have an illness. Having hair cut by a barber: Big profit in business. Having a shave at the barber's: Loss of money. Having haircut and shave by a female barber: Will have good clothes.

BAREFOOT:

A man going barefooted: Postponement of success. A woman going barefooted: All her life, will never have a lasting love. Children going barefooted: Shame and sorrow. Only the feet being bare: Expect trouble and difficulty. Feet and legs to knees being bare: Dishonor in social life. Feet and legs to hips being bare: Will serve a small prison term.

BARGAIN:

Of bargaining: Should trust only your own opinions. Being cheated out of a bargain: Own home will be robbed. Having made a good bargain: Advancement within position. Others making a good bargain: Have loyal friends.

BASHFUL:

Being bashful: Will have a pleasant time at a large party. Having bashful children: Joy. Having bashful friends: Warning of troubles ahead.

BASKET:

Of a full basket: Good business ventures. Having a full

basket: Will make plenty of money. Having an empty basket: Will lose money. Other people's baskets: Family will increase in number.

BATH:

Of a bathtub: Will become very angry. Being in a bathtub: Anxiety. Taking a bath in ice water. Disgrace. Taking a bath in cold water: Big sorrow. Taking a bath in warm water: Will be separated from a loved one. Taking a bath in lukewarm water: Wealth. Taking a bath early in the morning: Will soon get married. Taking a bath at noot: Pleasures and good health. Taking a bath in the evening: A false friend is nearby. Taking a bath at bedtime: Will surrender to sweetheart. Preparing a bath: Will have a fight with some person. Preparing a bath for yourself: Serious illness. Preparing a bath for mate: Will realize high ambitions. Preparing a bath for loved one: Will have a luxurious life. Preparing a bath for children: Happiness. Preparing a bath for sweetheart: This love affair will break up. Getting in a bathtub clothed: Will quarrel with your lover. Being in a bathtub with the one you love: will receive an inheritance. Undressing but not getting in the tub: Will have love troubles. An empty bathtub: Will have business worries.

BATHING:

Bathing in the open: Success and good health. Bathing in clear water: Success in business. Bathing in dirty water: Expect difficulties. Bathing in muddy water: DEath of a relative. bathing in the open sea: Will receive a big fortune. Bathing in water choked with weeds: Death of an animal. Bathing in a river: Unusually good business ahead. Bathing in a canal: Will be very rich. bathing in a lake: Will be unhappy. Bathing in a swimming pool. Illness. Bathing in a marsh: Will be very unlucky. Bathing at a bathhouse: Will have ulcers. Bathing in a cascade of water: Present projects will be a failure. Bathing in a house: Anxiety. Going bathing at sea with your mate: Will realize own hopes. Going bathing at sea with children: Happiness within the family. Going bathing at sea with a loved one: Will have luxurious life. Going bathing at sea with a sweetheart: End of this love affair. Going bathing in the nude: Will receive an inheritance. Going bathing with clothes on: Will have an argument.

BATS:

A gray bat: Will have an easy life. A black bat: Will quarrel and disaster awaits. A white bat: Recovery of a sick person. Many bats: Death within the family.

BATTLE:

Of a battle: Will enter into risky ventures. Watching a battle: Will be persecuted. A naval battle: Will be triumphant. A battle on land. Will live a long life. A battle with fists: Double cross in love affairs. Being defeated in battle: Unwise business dealings of others will hurt you. Fighting a battle alone: Things will turn out right for you. Winning a battle: Will have a good future.

BAZAAR:

Of a bazaar: Luck and prosperity. Being at a bazaar: Happiness in love. Buying things at a charity bazaar: Will realize high ambitions. People selling things at a charity bazaar: Will receive a proposal.

BEADS:

Stringing beads: Will receive favors from a wealthy person. Buying beads: Will have false friends. Scattering beads: Loss of reputation. Losing beads: Will be molested. Counting beads: Will have much joy and deep content. Finding beads: Misery and tears. Selling beads: Beware of untrue friends. Fishing beads: Scarcity.

BEARD:

Having a beard: Financial distress. A very short beard: Riches. A man having a full beard: Unexpected success to come. A very long beard: Will receive plenty of money. A married woman dreaming of a man with a beard: Will soon leave husband. A pregnant woman dreaming of a man with a beard: Will give birth to a son. A girl dreaming of a man with a beard: Will soon marry the one she loves. Pulling off own beard: Ruin and poverty. Others pulling off a beard: Will have to pay creditors. Cutting and shaving the beard: LOss of money. Cutting the beard of someone you know: Security. Someone else washing your beard: Grief. Washing own beard: Anxiety. Having a handsome beard: Complete success in own enterprises. Having a curly beard: Will make the impression you desire. Not having a beard: Big gain in business. Making a beard smaller: Danger of losing wealth. Losing hairs from the beard: loss of a relative. A black beard: Promising success in business. A reddish beard: Provocation. A white beard: Very big prosperity. A brown beard: Misery. A gray beard: Loss of money. The beard turning gray: Will suffer from gossip and slander. A very thin beard: Death of a member of the family. A married woman dreaming of having a small beard: Divorce. Unmarried woman dreaming of having a small beard: Gambling losses. A pregnant woman dreaming of having a small beard: Abortion. A widow woman dreaming of having a small beard: Loss of an estate. A young girl dreaming of having a small beard: Matrimony.

BEAST:

Talking to animals: Hardship and misfortune. Beasts making babbling noises: Will suffer grief. Beasts fighting: Sickness. Beasts scuffling: Cruel suffering. Being pursued by beasts: Vexation caused by enemies. Beasts starting a fight: Will be molested by friends. Beasts running: Serious illness.

BEATEN:

Being beaten: Unhappiness in home relations. Others being beaten: Loss of money. A dog being beaten: Fidelity. A cat being beaten: Treachery. A horse being beaten: Hapiness. A snake being beaten: Triumph.

BEATING:

Beating a husband or a wife: Both will be very happy. Married people dreaming of beating someone: Will live a peaceful life. Bachelors dreaming of beating someone: Good fortune in love affairs. Unmarried girls dreaming of beating men: Success in love. A lover beating his mistress: The affair will be ended. A woman beating her suitor: Big triumph in love. A husband beating his wife: Happiness and a comfortable home. A wife beating her husband: Longlasting marriage. A man beating a woman who is not his wife: Favorable business. Parents beating their children: Unexpected good affairs. Beating the children of strangers: long illness. A man beating a sweetheart: Future engagement. A woman beating her sweetheart: Happiness in love. Beating a friend: Contentment. Being beaten by a friend: Unhappiness in love. A bachelor slapping someone on the face: Will soon fall in love. A married man slapping someone on the face: Marriage will last forever. A married woman slapping a man on the face: She is faithful to husband. Beating a pig or other animals: Damages in own affairs.

BEAUTIFUL:

Being beautiful: Illness. Other people who are beautiful: They will be an invalid. A man dreaming of a beautiful woman: Treason. Of a beautiful girl: joy and happiness. A woman dreaming of a handsome man: Love will not last long. A man being with his beautiful wife: Pleasing time in love. A man being with a beautiful woman: Will have agreeable pastimes.

BED:

Resting comfortably in own bed: Will have security and love. A bed made neatly: Will have a contented heart. Having clean white sheets on a bed: Will have cause to worry. Having clean colored sheets on a bed: Arrival of unexpected guests. Making a bed: Change of residence to come. An empty bed: Death of a friend. Sitting on own bed: Will have an early marriage. Being in a strange bed: Good turn of events in own affairs. Remaining in bed for a long time: Misfortune is nearby. Being in bed but unable to sleep: Will soon become ill. A bed being in disorder: Secrets will be discovered. Being sick in bed: Complications will develop or death. A stranger being in your bed: Matrimonial unfaithfulness. Being in bed in a hotel room: Friends will visit you unexpectedly. A bed for camping: Will purchase real estate. Burning a bed: Secrets will be divulged. Old people going to bed: Death is near at hand. Children going to bed: Will people going to bed: Death is near at hand. Children going to bed: Will be unfortunate.

BED CLOTHES:

Many bed clothes: Will receive a big inheritance. Purchasing bed clothes : Peril is ahead. Wealth people having many bed clothes: Loss of money. Wealth people dreaming of bed clothes: Improvement in life. Poor people dreaming of bed clothes: Financial condition will be good.

BED ROOM:

Of own bedroom: Changes in own affairs. Someone's luxurious bedroom: Delays in present affairs. A bedroom in an apartment: Concealment of family secrets. Sleeping in a hotel bedroom: Stupid gossip will be passed around. Sleeping in the bedroom of a friend: Will become drunk.

BELLY:

Of own belly: Health and joy. Having pains in the belly: Will have business disturbances. A swollen belly: Serious illness. A very large belly: Enlargement of own fortune. A big belly and not being pregnant: Beware of untrue friends. A small belly: Free yourself of bad affairs. Unmarried woman dreaming of a big belly: Will soon be married.

BENEFITS:

Conferring benefits of others: Happiness. Receiving benefits from family: Big joy. Friends being beneficial: A mystery will be solved.

BERRIES :

of berries: Will enjoy social activities of a happy nature. Picking berries: Financial gains. Eating berries: Abundant means. Buying berries: Important and very beneficial events to come.

BET:

Of making bets: Do not trust own opinions too much. Others making bets: Don't allow opinions of others to interfere with you. Winning a bet: Will have a change for the better. Losing a bet: An enemy is seeking your ruin.

BIG:

. Being a very big person: Riches and honors. Being extra big and tall: Will be loved by the opposite sex. Having a high rank in society: Persecution. Being a big talker around women: Honor and dignity. Being visited by big people: Abundance.

BILLS:

Paying bills: Immediate financial gains. Not paying bills: Danger in business. Having overdue bills: Others are speaking evil of you. Being solicited to pay bills: Are disliked by your boss.

BINOCULARS:

Owing binoculars: Will have happiness in th future. Men looking through binoculars: Happiness. Women looking through binoculars: Will be greatly compensated in life. Military people using binoculars: Will be greatly compensated in life. Military people using binoculars: Will damaged in personal affairs. Viewing a loved one through binoculars: Loss of a distant relative. Being watched through binoculars: Think carefully before acting. Buying binoculars: A woman of poor morals is nearby.

BIRTH:

A married woman giving birth to a child: Joy will be hers. Single woman giving birth to a child: Will be abandoned by her lover. Divorced woman giving birth to a child: Will inherit a large legacy. Widow giving birth to a child: Will be guilty of foolish actions. Assisting with the birth of a child: Joy and prosperity. Assisting with the birth of a child (twins) or triplets: Very large success. Assisting with the birth of a dead child: Failure of present projects. Assisting with a

Caesarean birth: Will have a dangerous illness. Birth endangering life of pregnant woman: Will hear news of a marriage soon. Pregnant woman dreaming of having a boy: Complete success in enterprises. Pregnant woman dreaming of having a girl: Social presures followed by pain. Man dreaming of wife having twins: Wealth and riches to come soon. A father receiving news of a birth while away: Good wishes. the birth of an eagle: Will have a very prosperous future. The birth of a cat or other animals: Death of an enemy. Of a birth occurring: Prosperity and abundance. Giving birth to a child: Good fortune. Only one baby being born: Will be treated with force. Twins being born: Will have good luck in affairs. The birth of close relatives: Abundant means. Birth of fish: Will soon rain.

BIRTHDAY:

Of own birthday: Good results in financial matters. Relative's birthday: Good business affairs. Friend's birthday: Will benefit shortly. Sweetheart's birthday: Abundance of money soon coming. Wife's birthday: Good times are coming. Husband's birthday; Abundant means. Children's birthday: Approaching money.

BITS:

Of a bite: Are about to sustain a loss. Biting someone else: Will be embarrassed. Biting the tongue: Loss of consideration from other people. Being bitten by a woman: A jealous person is nearby. Being bitten by a man: Beware of quarrels. Being bitten by an animal: Will have troubles over love affairs. Being bitten several times: Are being slandered by other people.

BITTER:

Testing something bitter: Will have a rash all over the body. Taking bitter medicine: Will quarrel with help. Feeling bitter towards you: Will quarrel with other people.

BLANKET:

Wealthy person dreaming of buying new blankets: Improvement of conditions. Poor people dreaming of buying new blankets: Success. Having old blankets: Good news is on the way.

BLEEDING:

Own nose bleeding: Will be held in contempt by others. Others' nose bleeding: Will encounter opposition. Bleeding a little from own body: Achievement of own desires. Bleeding heavily from own body: Will fall into a trap. Blood flowing onto the floor: Good success.

BLESSING:

Receiving a blessing: Will be forced into a marriage. Children receiving a blessing: Happiness. Family receiving blessings: Joy without profit. Receiving a blessing from a priest: Will be very fortunate. Several others receiving blessings: Will have a happy family.

BLINDFOLDED:

A woman being blindfolded: Will bring disappointment to others. A man being blindfolded: Will be a widower. Being among blindfolded people: Persecution by a friend. Other people being blindfolded: Will have a troubled conscience.

BLOSSOM:

All sorts of trees blossoming: Joy and comfort. Own

flowers blossoming: Danger through a secret. Neighbour's flowers blossoming: Triumph over enemies. Blossoming trees and flowers growing: will enjoymuch recreation.

BLOT:

Making a blot on clean white paper: Will sleep in a strange bed. Making a blot on colored paper: will travel in near future. Blotting an important document: Change for the better. Blotting the writing on a check: Happiness is assured.

BLUE:

Buying clothes of blue color: will have a vigourous mind. the color of the blue sky: Big love for children. Navy blue color: Prosperity through other people. Azure blue color: Promotion in own employment. Any other shade of blue: Comfortable happy married life.

BLUNDER:

Of a blunder: Will do unexpextedly well in new undertaking. Blundering about clumsily: Success in all affairs. Other people blundering: Accord among frineds. Retalives blundering: Good times are coming.

BLUSH:

Blushing with shame: Will be obligated to offer explanations. Blushing with pleasure: will have to take laxative. Blushing when caught in wrongdoing: Will be loved by an old woman. Children blushing: Will breakup with best friends. Sweathearts blushing: they will get married before date set.

BODY:

Of own body: Happiness. The body of a woman: People

are flirting with this woman. The body of a man: Good business ventures. The body of children: Will undertake a journey. The body of a deformed person: Will have good fortune ahead.

BOIL:

Boiling water: Must moderate passions. Boiling food: Will have such hapiness. Boiling coffee: Will have emotional sorrow. Boiling soups: Financial gains.

BOMB:

Of a bomb: Will receive dreadful news. Hearing the sound of a bomb: Happiness within the family. Having been injured by a bomb: Serious disaster ahead.

BOMBARDMENT:

Of a bombardment: Will have misfortune. Having been bombarded: Will have an unhappy marriage. Others being bombarded: Deception in love matters.

BOOK:

Books in a library: Will have an unexpected experience. Books at home: Happiness. Reading a book: Will lose good friends. Reading mystery books: Will receive consolation from friends. Reading science books: Big joy. Reading stories and detective books: will lead a quiet life. Reading religious books: Contentment. Reading schoolbooks: Prosperity. Binding books: Will find something that was hidden away. Writing books: Will waste time and money.

BOOTS:

Wearing boots: Will have small amount of good business. Buying new boots: Business will be very good.

Having new boots: Can rely on the faithfulness of servants. Old boots: will meet with difficulties. Having brown boots: Will have good luck. Old boots hurting the feet: Loss of money due tooown carelessness. Other people with new boots: Danger in love matters.

BOTTLE:

A full bottle: Prosperity. An emply bottle: Misfortune. Spilling the contents of a bottle: Expect domestic worries. A bottle of wine: Will be in a bad humor. An emply flask: Will be disappointed in love. A bottle full of loquor: Will be divoroed. An empty bottle of loquor: Own affairs. will be good. A full bottle of perfume: Will enjoy much happiness. An empty bottle of perfume: Love affairs are on the focks.

BOUQUET:

A beautiful bouquet: A begacy is ahead in the future. A withered bouquet: Illness and ensuing death. Receiving a bouquet: Much pleasure in life. Giving a bouquet: Lover is constent. Keeping a bouquet of flowers: Will receive a marriage proposal. Throwing away a bouquet: Sepration from a freind. Preparing a bouquet of flowers: Will be married soon. Receiving several bouquets of flowrs: will be married soon. Receiving several bouquets: will have a faithful love. Receiving a small bouquet: Joy that will not last a long time.

BOX:

Having a box: Will go out of business. Tying a box: Financial losses. Opening a box: Will take a long journey. Opening a full box: Will receive a marriage proposal. Opening an empty box: Plants will be upset. A church charity box: Will have misery. A strong box: Will be cheated. Robbing a strongbox: Will lose entire fortune.

BOY:

Of boys: Increase in the· family. Boys fighting: Will make a good resolution. Boys jumping: will collect money. Boys boxing: something bad will occur very soon. Having a boy: A woman will soon become prgnant. A boy being sick: Obstacles are ahead. Reescuing a boy from danger: Will rise to eminence. A boy being killed: Misery caused by parents. a crippled boy: Troubles are ahead. Adopting a boy: Other children will dislike the adopted son. A young boy: Will soon be married. Several young boys: Will receive good news. A young boy dating a young girl: Must keep house in better order. A young boy working in a store: Will enjoy good business. A young boy securing work at a store: Unhappiness.

BRAIN:

Of brains: Will have an accident. Having a sane brain: Great knowledge will bring good results in affairs. Having a sick brain: Loss of money. Having a brain tymor: You do not have a good reputation. Relatives having a poor brain: Dangers ahead in the future. Other people having a sane brain: Will be a very intellegent person. Having a brain operation: Are a very passionate person. Young people dreaming of eating brains: Will fall in love. Elderly people dreaming of eating brains: Good health. Performing a brain operation: Everything will go well in the future. Friends having a brain operation: Will find a valueable hidden object. Enemies having a brain operation: Will enjoy good earnings.

BRASSIERE:

Of own brassiere: Another person is enjoying what you desired. The brassiere of your wife: Avoid rivals. The brassiere of a sweatheart: Temptation will come. The brassiere of others: Will be jilted by lover. Buying a brassiers: Will have a vigourous mind. Losing a brassiere: Will find someone new for whom you will care.

BRAVERY:

Acting with bravery: Will have a nervous illness. Being with cut bravery: Are apt to underestimate yourself. Showing courage and bravery: A friend holds a secret enmity against you. Other acting with bravery: Troubles ahead.

BREAD:

Of bread crumbs: Will receive a gift. Baking bread: Will meet with success. Eating bread: Will be helped by friends. A hot loaf of bread: Wealth and honor will be yours. Stale bread: Domestic trouble. A very hard loaf of bread: Physical well being and comfort. Having several loaves of breads: Honor. Buying bread: Big success. Eating white breead: Will make a big profit. Eating dark bread Contentment. Eating black bread: Business losses. Carrying several loaves of bread: Will have some financial damages.

BREAKFAST:

Preparing breakfast: Misery and illness. Eating breakfast alone: Will commit some folly. Eating breakfast with others: Will soon receive money. Having breakfast in a coffee shop: Will have a new sweetheart. Having breakfast in the home of others: Will take a trip before long.

BREAST:

Having a beautiful breast: Big joy ahead. Resting on someone's breast: true and loyal friendship. The breast of a woman: Wishes will be fratified. The breast of a man: Will soon be married. A breast covered with hair: Success in love. A woman having hair on her breast: Her husband will soon pass away. A baby sucking at the breast: Will enjoy lasting happiness. Young people having breast wounded: Will have splendid future. Old people having breast wounded: Will have misfortune. Breast being wounded with a sword during a duel: Bad news. Breast being wounded with a knife in a fight: Good friendship. Brest being wounded by a gun will make plenty of money.

BRIDE:

A young woman being a bride: Will soon have a large legacy. Kissing a bride: Will have many friends and much joy. Being kissed by a bride: Will have good health. A bride being pleased with her gown: Will have many children. A bride being displeased with her gown: Disappointment in love.

BRIDEGROOM:

A bridegroom having a rich bride: Loss of the father A bridegroom having a beautiful bride: Loss of the mother. A bridegroom having a young bride: Sickness within the family. A bridegroom having an elderly bride: Abundant means.

BRIDGE:

Crossing a bridge: Will have a change of business of accupation. A man crossing a bridge: Will have a change of home. A woman crossing a bridge: Will have social activities of happy nature. A single person crossing a bridge: Will soon be married.

A bridge that opens in the center: Will pardon enemies. A red bridge: Danger ahead. A bridge burning: Will lose some friends. A bridge falling while walking on it: Financial losses. Falling from a bridge: Affairs will be bad. A bridge being built: Will make good business. Crossing a bridge under repairs: Will have many troubles. Crossing a damaged bridge:

Be careful in making new plans. Driving over a bridge: Abandon present plans. Others crossing a bridge: Will have delays in own business.

BRIEFCASE:

Having a briefcase: Will have riches for a short time. A briefcase full of papers: Will neglect some of own business. A briefcase without any papers: Good results in enterprises. Losing a briefcase: Will make good business. Finding a breifcase: Failure in all affairs.

BROOM:

Having a new broom: Will make plenty of money. Having an old broom: Beware of false friends. Throwing away an old broom: Good luck to one for whom you care. Hitting something with a broom: will have a change for the better.

BROTHER:

A man dreaming of his brother: Expect quarrels. A woman dreaming of her brother: Much domestic happiness. Quarreling with a brother: Big fortune. A brother dying: Destruction of enemies. A brother getting married: Family quarrels.

BROTHER-IN-LAW:

Of a brother-in-law: Are being taken advantage of by relatives. Marrying a brother-in-law: will recover from an illness. Flirting with a brother-in-law: Failure of enemies. Having several brother-in-law: Financial gains.

BROWN:

Of the color brown: Big friendship. Brown material: Will

be doublecrossed by employees. Brown hair: A change in life will soon come. Buying brown clothes: Joy without profit.

BUBBLES :

Of bubbles: Will escape a present peril. Creating bubbles: Avoid wastefulness or may lose sweetheart. Bubbles in a bathtub: Will find a protector. Bubbles from boiling water: Dignity and distinction.

BUCKLE:

A woman having a buckle unfastened: Troubles and difficulties ahead. A man unfastening a woman's buckle: Marriage will take place soon. Having a fancy buckle: Will have a change for the better. Buying a buckle: Avoid rivals. A broken buckle: An enemy is seeking your destruction.

BUGS:

Of bugs: Success in business or worldly affairs. Many bugs: Will have gold and silver given to you. Killing bugs: Will have money. Others killing bugs: Will go to prison. Having bugs in the house: Will have a great deal of money. Having bugs outside the house: Do not place blame on friends. Having bugs in the bedding: Prosperity beyond fondest hopes.

BULLDOG:

Owing a bulldog: Advancement is own position. A bulldog being in the street: Will find a big protector. Having a bulldog in the house: Good news from an absent friend. Buying a bulldog: Happiness is assured. Selling the puppies of a bulldog: Anenemy is seeking your ruin.

BURDEN:

Carrying a burden: Will be dependent upon other people. Other people carrying a burden: Expect a large inheritance. Children carrying a burden: Advancement in own position. Friends carrying a burden: Financial gains.

BURGLAR:

A burglar being in own house: Beware of treachery. A burglar coming into the house at night: Approching troubles. Catching a burglar red-handed: Will gain good fortune. Burglars having stolen valueable things: Good investments.

BURIAL:

Attending the burial of a friend: Are expecting an inharitance. Attending the burial of a relative: Will be married soon. Attending the burial of a relative when married: Divorce. Attending the burial of mother or father: Good financial speculations.

BURST:

Of bursting: Will have amusement and joy. Having burst something: Will receive an inheritance. Friends bursting some thing: Good results in business. Enemies bursting something: Give credit where credit is due.

BURYING:

Of burying: Will have good real estate holdings. Burying a steel pan: Unhapiness. Burying a pot of gold: Will have an accident. Burying stolen property in a box: Will have a happy life. Burying money: Dissolution of hopes.

BUSINESS:

Doing business: untruthful gossip. Beginning a good

business: Must fight for good results. Making money in business: Will receive money from a friend. Losing money in business: Will lose your temper.

BUTTER:

Eating butter: Happiness. Having plenty of butter: Good luck of some kind to come. Purchasing butter: Will have a change for the butter. Cooking with butter: Will be fortunate in business. Selling butter: Avoid financial speculations. Making butter in own house: Will receive a present. Frying with butter: Will have a new admire.

BUTTERFLY:

A butterfly flitting from flower to flower: Great prosperity. A beautifully colored butterfly in the sunshine: Happiness in love. A butterfly being in the house: Will have some slight trouble. A young woman dreaming of a butterfly: Will have a happy marriage. Catching a butterfly: Infidelity. Killing a butterfly: Will receive a gift. Chasing a butterfly: Are surrounded by unfortunate influences.

BUTTOCKS:

Of own buttocks: fortune is ahead. The buttocks of a man: Good business will soon come. The buttocks of a woman: Happiness and love. The buttocks of a baby: Family re-union. The buttocks of animals: Will soon have money. The buttocks of a dog: Will soon be visited by thieves.

BUTTONS:

A single man dreaming of sewing on buttons: Delay in love affairs. A woman dreaming of sewing on buttons: Will receive unexpected money. Losing buttons: Secret enmity of some person. Buying buttons: Will have a vigorous mind.

BUY:

Buying diffrent articles : Troubles ahead in finanacial matters. Buying food: Will have an average success. Buying vegetables: Family quarrels. buying fruits: Misfortune in love affairs. Buying clothes: Big success ahead. Buyimng facse powder: Will be extravagant in spending money. Buying things for children: Will have much good luck.

C

CAB:

Riding in a cab alone: Are engaged in a suitable hobby. Riding in a cab with friends: Discovery of a secret. A man riding in a cab with a woman: Name will be connected with scandal. A woman riding in a cab alone: Will enjoy average success. Riding in a cab at Night: Are kepinmg secrets from friends. Riding in a cab at night: Are keeping secrets from friends. Riding in a cab in the rain: Correspondence with friends living abroad. Riding in a cab to met sweetheart: Weaknesses will be known. Riding in a cab with wife: Will have a long life. Riding in cab with children: Hapiness within the family. Riding in a cab with relatives: Will encounter gossip in the future.

CABBAGE:

Eating cabbage: Uncertain livelihood. Buying cabbage: good health and long life. Boiling cabbage: suitable work and good news. Growing caabbage: Be cautious in business affairs. making a cabbage salad: Abundant means.

CABIN:

Bcing in the cabin of a ship: Domestic troubles. Being in a cabin at the beach: Love affairs. Being in a country cabin: Good days ahead. Being in a cabin with a lover: Dealth of an enemy. Being in a cabin with friends: Danger in love matters.

CACKLE:

Hearing a hen cackle at dawn: Warning that cafe is needed. Hearing a hen cackle at noon: Fights between relatives. Hearing a hen cackle in the evening: Big peril.

CAGE:

An empty cage: A member of the family will elope. A cage full of birds: Untold wealth. Only one bird in a cage: Will have many lovely children. Two birds in a cage: Will have succesfull love affairs. Three birds in a cage: Engagement will be broken. Wild animals in a cage: Danger of going to prison.

CAKE:

Being a cake: will have a luck turn of events. Eating a piece of cake: will lose sweetheart. Buying a cake: Will enjoy the affection of a friend. A woman dreaming of eating her wedding cake: Big peril. Serving cake to friends: Are confronted with insurrrmoundtable obstacles.

CALL:

A single person dreaming of hearing name called: Will soon fail in love. A married person dreaming of hearing name called: Will soon fail in love. A married person dreaming of hearing name called: Will soon divorce. Calling someone else: Look for important news. Being called by several people: Will be insulted by a relative.

CALM:

Calming yourself: Will have many adventures. Calming angry people: Illness of children. Calming the screaming of one suffering: you have a violent temper. Calming husband or wife: Will have a violent family quarrel. Calming sweetheart:

Sickness. Calming friends: Loss of money. Calming othere people: Misfortune in love affairs. Ordering others to be calm: Will be loved and ridiculed.

CAMERA:

Owning a camera: Will receive disagreeable news. Looking into a camera: Will be decived. Buying a camera: Will be joy without profit. Receiving a camera as a gift: Will have love troubles.

CARDS:

playing cards: Will take a trip abroad. Other people playing cards: Will have quarrels soon. Playing cards and winning: Troubles ahead. Playing cards and losing: Good business ventures arc faraway. Being a card dealer: Bad news.

CARESS:

A mother caressing her children: Anxious days because of illness. A wife caressing her husband happy events. A husband caressing his wife: Will have good earnings. Sweethearts careessing each other: Will receive dreadful news.

CARPENTER:

Being a carpenter at work: Success in financial matters. Hiring a carpenter: Unexpexted good news. A carpenter working busily: Will overcome difficulties. A carpenter fixing the house: finanacial security.

CARPET:

Several carpets: Danger for the one who owns the carpet. Making carpets: Big happiness. Buying a carpet: A mystery will be solved. A carpet burning: Be on gurad against spiteful gossip. Being in a carpeted room: Expect good news. Exchanging a carpet for a new one: Dissatisfaction in love. Laying a carpet: Big catastrophe ahead.

CARROTS:

Of carrots : profit trrough inheritanvce. Having carrots in the home: Will have plenty of money. Growing carrots: accord among friends. Eating carrots: Joy without profit. Cooking carrots: Abundance.

CARRY:

Of being carried by anyone: Will have an uncertain future. Being carried by a man: Will have anxious days because of illness. Carrying a woman: Difficulties will soon be overcome. Being carried by a woman: Will have new love affairs. Being carried by a poor person: Happiness.

CASHIER:

Of a cashier: Big joy without profit. Being a cashier: Expect financial worry. Watching a cashier: Freedom from want. Several cashiers at a bank: Are being deceived.

CAT:

Of brown, white or gray cats: Are being deceived by a trusted person. A black cat: Illness is near. Defending yourself from a cat: Will be robbed. Cats playing: Will be visited at home by enemies. A furious cat: Will have argument with lover. A cat with her kittens: Unhapiness in marriage. Being scratched by a cat: Someone is seeking your downfall. A pregnant cat: Will be robbed. A cat eating rats: Will receive payment of money loaned. A cat sleeping: Small success. A cat eating her food: Divorce. A cat fighting with a dog: Will have quarrels with neighbors. Hitting a cat: will fall into bad company. Many cats and dogs: Loss of profits in a business deal. A cat being on the roof. Will be unsuccessful in affairs. A cat delivering kittens: Divorce is near at hand.

CATALOGUE:

Of a catalogue : good business ahead. Receiving a catalogue: Will lose money. Making a selection from a catalogue: Attempt to be diligent in future. Cataloguing store merchandise: Will enjoy large gambling winnings. Cataloguing machinery: Loss in personal affairs. cataloguing documents: Small unhappiness. Cataloguing clothes and shoes: Friends. Will place blame upon you.

CATERPILLAR:

Of this piece of machinery: May suffer from malicious tongues. Owning a caterpillar: Watch own actions. Working with a caterpillar: Good business ahead.

CATHEDRAL:

The interior of a cathedral: Take care of own business. The outside of a cathedral: Good fortune. Being in a cathedral: Will receive honors.

CATTLE:

Many cattle : Prosperity according to the number of cattle. Black cattle: Troubles ahead in business. Cattle of other colors: Prosperity in business. Driving cattle: Must work hard. Fat cattle: Will have a fruitful year. Lean cattle: Will be in want of provisons. Being followed by cattle: Loss in business. Being rich and owning cattle: Disgrace and loss in business. Being poor and owning cattle: Good profits.

CAULIFLOWER:

Of CAULIFLOWER : Good health and comfortable home life. Eating cauliflower: Joy and honor. Growing cauliflower: Treason by a friend. Buying cauliflower: Will have good health.

CEILING:

The ceiling of own room being damaged: happiness. A cracked ceiling: Will have troubles caused by a friend. Repairing a ceiling: Good times are coming.

CEMETERY:

Of a cemetery: Will conquer all things. Being in a cemetery: Will soon have propertity. A bride passing a cemetery on way to marriage: She will lose husband. Children gathering flowers in a cemetery. Coming prosperity. Elderly people putting flowers in a cemetery: Will have no grief.

CERTIFICATE:

Receiving a certificate : Do not see things from others' point of view. Giving a certificate: people will recognize your innocence. Receiving a stock certificate: Finanacial losses.

CHAINS:

Of iron chains: Will escape from some difficulty. Cutting a chain: Will have worries for a short time. Wearing a chain: Expect bad days in the near future. A gold chain around a woman's neck: Good fortune with friend or lover. A person wearing chains in jail: Business will be bad. Succeeding in breading the chains: Will be free of social engagements. Others in chains: Ill fortune for them. Being bound in chains: Will soon be releved of burdens.

CHAIR:

Of an empty chair : Will receive news from an absent friend. Sitting in a comfortable arm chair: Will have prosperity. Sitting in a chair and being moved by others: Will receive high honors.

CHALK:

Of chalk : Disappointment in some cherished hope. Buying chalk: Will have a long life. Handling chalk: Will soon be married.

CHALLENGE:

Being challenged : Will reconcile with enemies. Challenging someone to a duel: Immidiate death of a relative. Challenging someone to boxing match: Will be a public shame to community. Others challenging: Be prudent in the future.

CHAMPAGNE:

Drinking champagne : Will be unfortunate in love affairs. Buying Champagne : Big happiness. Being at a champagne party: Will be happy with lover.

CHANDELIER:

Church chandeliers : Will go to prison. Chandeliers with candles hanging from the ceiling: Prosperity. Chandeliers with globes hanging from the ceiling: Wealth. A table chandelier with candles: Misfortune in love affairs.

CHANGE:

Of conditions in life changing: Damages to present condition. A woman changing her sex: A son will be born to bring honor to family. A man changing his sex: Great family dishonor. Other people changing their sex: Infirmity. Changing course while driving: Many troubles ahead. Changing clothes: will receive a large damage.

CHARMS:

Of a charm : Beware of jealous Friends. Wearing a charm: Will have an important decision to make soon. Buying a charm to ward off evil : Will mary soon. Selling a charm : Unhappiness. Receiving a charm as a gift: Will soon experience many ups and downs.

CHASTISE:

Chastising the children : Happy and prosperous life. Being chastised: Will be unfortuneate in financial matters. Others being chasised: Are being deceived. Chastising another: Will have illtempered husband or wife. Being chastised by others: Troubles ahead with business partner. Being chastised by the family: Triumph over enemies.

CHEATING:

Of cheating : Take care of own self. Having been cheated : Don't trust false friends. Cheating in a gambling game: Are confronted with insurmountable obstacles. Having been cheated in gambling: Use caution in business affairs. Others cheating in gambling: An enemy is seeking your ruin.

CHECK:

Of checks : Financial gains. Having checks. A change in life will soon come. Giving a check: Accord among friends.

CHEEKS:

Beautiful cheeks: Joy and contentment. Rosy cheeks:

Long life. Pale cheeks: Will be in need of provisions. Name cheeks: Will have good health. A woman dreaming of her own cheeks: Will be loved very much. A man dreaming of his own cheeks: will have plenty of joy.

CHEERING:

Of cheering : Will have bad luck. Others cheering: Avoid spending too much money. Hearing the sound of cheering: Be careful of own actions.

CHESS:

Playing chess : Difficulties ahead in your path. Others playing chess : Fortune will depend upon results of the game. Winning a game of chess. Approaching money. Losing a game of chess: Troubles ahead.

CHICKENS:

Of one fine chicken : Will be fortunate in love. Several chickens: Will have many good friends. Chickens laying eggs: Joy and contentment. A chicken sitting on her eggs: Joy and happiness. A chicken with her chicks: Will receive a favor. Eating chicken: will be afflicted. Cooking chicken: will make considerable money. Killing a chicken: Profit.

CHILDREN:

Of children : A woman will become pregnant soon. Several children : Will have abundance in life. Little children: Disappointment and sorrow. Pretty children: Happy and successful career. Children at play: Good deeds will bear fruit. Children falling: Loss in business. Having many children of your own : Sucess in business. Adopting children: own children will dislike those adopted. Children being killed: Misery caused by parents. Talking to own children: Losses in business. Children being sick: obstacies are ahead. A child being crippled: Troubles await. Children studying: Will have a great deal of fun. A mother holding her child against her breast: Child will have bad health. A child with her nurse: Mother will have another child. Being a bastard child: Will have trouble raising all your children. A man dreaming of being with his child: Riches.

CHIN:

Of own chin: Good business in the future. Having a large chin: Will receive money. Having a beautiful chin: Poverty. Other people having a double chin: Will be complemented for doning good. Other people hurtig their chin: Good success.

CHOCOLATES:

Of chocolates candy: Will have a congenial occupation. Eating chocolates: Will receive a gift soon. Chocolate powder: Will have happiness and health. Buying chocolate: A short period of troubles will be followed by prosperity. Drinking chocolate: Will receive a marriage proposal.

CHRISTMAS:

Attending church on Christmas Day : Will receive God's blessings. Of Christmas : Will have happy family affairs. Being at a Chritmas party: Will have new good friends. Going Chritmas caroling: Great financial gains.

CIGRETTE:

Lighting a cigarette : Signifies new plans. Holding a half smoked cigrette in hands: Postponement of love. Smoking a cigarette to the end: Great success. A man and woman smoking cigarettes together: Conclusion of hopes.

CIRCUS:

Of a circus : Future unhappiness. Watching a circus performance: Loss of money. Taking children to a circus: Important and beneficial events to come.

CITY:

An inhabited city: Will be very rich. A large city: Will have much ambition. Seeing a city in the distance: Will have much success. A city burning: poverty. Being in a large city: Conclustion of hopes. Being in a small city: Must take good care of business. A city in ruins: Will have illness in the family. Going through a city: Will receive sad news from a friend. A beautiful losses.

CLAY:

Of clay : Own ideas are not clear. Working with clay : Will make good profits. Baking white clay: Good business prospects. Baking clay made from bricks: Big fortune ahead.

CLEAN:

Of cleaning : Embarrassment and quarrels. Cleaning yourself: Will have an everlasting friendship. Cleaning the teeth: Happiness. Cleaning children: Will achive victory over enemies. Cleaning house: Will receive news from an absent person.

CLIMBING:

Of climbing: Prosperity in business. Being unable to climb: Present efforts are not good enough. Climbing a mountain and reaching the summit: Will gain a fortune. Climbing but failing to reach the summit: Children plans will fail. Climbing a ladder to the top: Success in business. A ladder breading while climbing: Will have unexpected difficulties. Climbing a tree: Will receive a good position. Climbing the stairs of a house: Will overcome all abstacles.

CLOCK:

Hearing a clock strike the hours: Will be married soon. A church or ckity clock: Will enjoy a comfortable life. Having a wall clock: Will have happiness. Buying a wall clock: Will receive important business news. A clock being stopped: Will be spared from illness.

CLOTH:

Of cloth: Certain and secure profit. Linen cloth: Will make big earnings. Woolen cloth: Will make profits from own products. Velvet cloth: Will have an amorous conversation. Silk cloth: Big joy. Indian head cloth: Wrongdoings will be recognized. Frame for making cloth: Efforts are being wasted.

CLOTHES:

Having plenty of clothes: Troubles to come. Putting on clothes: Will receive good news from a stranger. Having no clothes on: Will receive plenty of money. Being partly dressed: Will have prosperity. Buying many clothes: Success in love.

CLOUDS:

Stormy and dark clouds: Will have many sorrows. Clouds passing away: Good fortune awaits. The sky being without clouds: Conclusion of own hopes. The sky being full of clouds: Arguments between business partner. Beautiful white clouds: Will become a miser. Very black clouds: Unhapiness. Downpour of rain from the clouds: Will have hard days ahead. Clouds clearing away: Will have a disagreeble attitude.

COACH:

Driving in a coach alone: May find yourself in difficulties. Driving in a coach with other people: Beware of treachery. Others driving a coach: Will be cheated by friends.

COAT:

Of a new coat : Are about to receive honors. Wearing a new coat: Beware of business troubles. Wearing an old coat: Prosperity is coming. Wearing a torn coat: Will receive big profits. Wearing another person's coat: Will be forced to seek a friend's help. Losing a coat: Will soon face financial ruin through speculation. Getting a coat dirty: Will lose a good friend.

COCK:

Hearing a cock crow : Great prosperity. Hearing a cock crow while asleep: Will receive good news. A cock being in the house: Will get married. Cocks fighting: Will have quarrels. A deed cock: Happiness in the family.

COCONUT:

A coconut tree : Will receive a fortune from parents. Buying coconut: Will have a love affair. Eating coconut: Will receive a large sum of money. A large tree full of coconuts: Women are gossiping.

COFFEE:

Making coffee : Great domestic happincss. Drinking coffee: Friends are discussing your wedding plans. Selling coffee: Financial losses. Buying coffee: Will have the best reputation in the business. Roasting coffee: Will have a visitor. Grinding coffee: Will overcome obstacles. Burning coffee: will be surrounded by evil. Pouring coffee: Security is forthcoming. Growing coffee: Great financial gains. Of a coffee shop: Will be deceived. Being in a coffee shop wsith good people: Highly considered by friends.

COINS:

Of coins: Great financial gains. Silver coins: Will have family troubles. A girl dreaming of silver coins: Will be jilted by her lover. Copper coins: Sickness. Nickel coins: Good work will be your fortune. Having gold coins in the hands: Misfortune.

Assembling all kinds of coins: Will receive good news. Counting coins: Will make a considerable profit. Stealing coins: Long sickness. Spending coins: Will risk failure in own plans. Finding coins: Good fortune in domestic affairs. Seeing all kinds of coins: promotion in own affairs.

COLD:

Feeling cold : Will have comfort and friendship. Having a bad cold: Security is forth coming. Mate having a cold: Abundant means. Children having a cold: Good times are coming.

COLLEGE:

A man or woman dreaming of being at college: Will receive bad news. Children going to college: Will be deceived. A woman dreaming of being inside a college: Will have a child. A man dreaming of being inside a college: A change in life to come soon. College buildings: Advancement will come to you.

COLORS:

Azalea : Big joy. Azure blue: Promotion in employment. Navy blue: Prosperity through other people. Black: Will have a very unfortunate time. Brown: Big friendship. Chrimson: Pleasant news from a friend. Gold: Will do business with people far away. Green: Good fortune in love affairs. Gray: Will receive a letter with good news. Mauve: Unhappiness. Orange: Fortune is near at hand. Pink: Glorious success. Purple: A joyful journey. Red: Quarrels with friends. Scarlet: Family quarrels. Silver: Will be fortunate in all dealings. White: Success in undertakings. Yellow: Important but bad changes will occur in own affairs. Several colors mixed together: You have false friends.

COMBING:

Combing own hair: Loss of a lover. Combing a young girl's hair: loss of friendship. Combing a boy's hair: Loss of money. Own hair being combed by others: Loss through someone trusted. Others combing their hair: Death of a relative. Hair being combed by a beautician: Honor. A beautician combing a rich woman's hair: Big fortune ahead.

COMFORT:

Living in comfort: Will receive bad news. Comforting children: Approahing money. Comforting other people: Will be fortunate in love. Being comforted by others: Happiness in love.

COMMUNICATE:

Communicating news : Security in business. Communicating orders: Will receive a grave injustice. Communicating bad news: Must rely upon own vigor. Communicating a secret: A change in life will soon come.

COMPLAIN:

Of complaining: Your become angry over unimportant

things too easily. Receiving complaints: Unhapiness. Complaining to others: There is no foundation for your hopes. Making a legal complaint: Important event, very beneficial.

CONDOLENCE: Receiving condolences: Death. Relatives giving condoleces: Unhapiness. Receiving condolences from people far away: Fortune. Offering condolences to the family of a dead person: Sickness.

CONGRATULATE:

Of congratulation : Must control passions. Receiving congratulations: Financial gains. Receiving congratulations: Financial gains. Receiving congratulations from influential people: Will enjoy good humor. Sending congratulations: Joy. Congratulations children: Approaching money. Congratulating others: Will have financial gains.

CONQUEST:

Of conquest: You expect too many favors from other people. Conquest of a woman: Must rely upon own good judgment. Conquest of a man: Avoid rivals. A victory: Triumph over enemies.

CONSTRUCTION:

Of construction: Will soon be molested. Constructing own home: Adversity. Constructing a home for others: Annoyance. Constructing an altar aat a church: Joy and consolation. Constructing tombs: Sickness. Constructing roads: Confusion in business affairs. Constructing docks: Will have many things on your mind. Constructing other things: Big profit ahead.

CONTRACT:

Drawing up a contract : Ill health. Making a purchase contract: Will have good health right upto death. Signing a contract of sale: Will be informed of an accident. Others making contracts: Will pass away very soon.

CONVERSATION:

Having a conversation with important people : Prosperity. Having a conversation with a group of people: Danger of rain. Having a conversation in the evening with a group: Gossip. Having a conversation with a priest: Hard days are ahead.

COOK:

Being a cook : Poverty. Being the cook at a restaurant: Will be cheated by friends. A maile cook: You expect too many favors of other people. A female cook: Great joy is in store. A young girl being a cook: Will soon become engaged.

COOKING:

Of cooking : Divorce is in sight. A man cooking: Will be invited to a party. A woman cooking: Beware of treachery. Others cokking: Will benefit in the near future. Several people cooking at the same time: Success in love.

COPULATE:

Of uniting in sexual intercourse: Happiness is assured. Others who are copulating: Abundant means. Yourself having sexual intercourse: Financial gains.

COSTUME:

Having several different costumes: Will live a long life. A man in a riding costume: A great effort will be required of you. A woman in a riding costume: Pleasant work and good news. The costume of a priest: Avoid rivals. Officers in uniforms: Will realize high ambitions. Having masquerade costumes: Important and very beneficial events to come. Others in different costumes: Will escape an unhappy position.

COTTAGE:

Living in a cottage : Better times to follow. Others living in a cottage: Will receive good news. An empty cottage: Loneliness and trouble.

COUGHING:

Of coughing: Indiscreet people are nearby. That you are coughing: Good health. Others Coughing: Good friendship. Children coughing: Good earnings.

COUNT:

Being a count: People are testing your character. Being in the company of a count: Do not speculate. Dealing with a count: Opposition in love affairs. Being friendly with a count: Will go to prison. Of a countess: Humiliation.

COUNTING:

Of counting : Ambitions will be satisfied. Counting money: Profit. Counting different items: Will suffer in own affairs. Counting and finding items missing: Result in business are unsure. Others counting: Joy. Counting men: Jealousy. Counting women: Will be tormented.

COURT:

Being in court: Important and very beneficial events to come. Going to court: Business losses. Having been in court:

Loss of prestige. Being requested to go to court: High consideration of others. being punished by a court: Travel and prosperity. Being acquitted by a court: Serious disaster is ahead.

COURTED:

Being courted: Doomed for disappointment. Courting someone else: Love affairs are not good. Being courted by a married person: Good luck. Being courted by an unmarried person: Will have happiness.

COUSIN:

Of a cousin: Relatives will ask you for help. Several of own cousins: Misfortune in love affairs. Being in the company of a cousin: Unexpected bad news. Being in the company of all your cousins: Danger in love.

COVER:

A table cover: Will receive a favor from important person. A bed cover: Great honors and good fame. Covering a wagon: Gossip. Coverings for furniture: Misery.

COW:

Of a cow: Prosperity. Several cows: Great prosperity in all ventures. Being chased by a cow but escaping: Watch own affairs carefully. Milking a cow: Will make good financial profits.

CREMATE:

Being cremated : Business failure if advice of others is followed. Requesting cremation at death: Abundant means. Mate being cremated: Poverty. Cremating a member of the family: Will receive a legacy. Others being cremated: Will possess abounding health.

CRIES:

Hearing happy and joyous cries : Export bad news. Hearing cries of trouble or distress: Everything will go well. Hearing cries of children: Change for the better.

CRIME:

Of a crime being committed : Another person is enjoying what you desired. Being caught while committing a crime: Will be sorely tempted. Others committing a crime: Danger through a secret.

CROCODILE:

Of a crocodile : You are in the grip of a deceitful people killing a crocodile: Warning of troubles ahead. Many crocodiles: Big catastrophe ahead.

CROSSROAD:

Unmarried people dreaming of a crossroad : Will soon be engaged. Married person dreaming of a crossroad: Loss of loved mate. Relatives being at a crossroad: Recovery from illness. Friends being at a crossroad. Secret enmity of some person.

CROW:

Of a crow: Disappointment in everything. Crows flying : Grief and misfortune. Crows flying over the head: Death in the family. A large flock of crows: Serious disaster ahead. Hearing the croak of crows: Illness of children. A woman dreaming of a crow: Death of her husband. A man dreaming of a crow: Death of his wife.

CROWD:

Of a crowd : Happiness is assured. being in a crowd: Advancement within position. Friends being in a crowd: New interests and surroundings. Enemies being in a crowd: Beware of jealous people.

CROWN:

Having a crown on the head: Will benefit through other people. Being crowned: Will have the friendship of important people. A royal crown: Will have plenty of happiness. Placing a crown on another's head. You are worthy of advancement. Having a gold crown on the head: Big protection of high officials. Having a crown of flowers: Big success. Having a crown of iron: Beware of business transactions. Having a crown of tin: LOss of fortune. Having a crown with a cross on it: Will benefit through a death.

CRYING:

Of crying : Domestic trials are on the way. Others crying: Will have to render aid to others. Memebers of the family crying: Will receive good news.

CUP:

Drinking from a cup: Good times are coming. Having an empty cup: Will have emotional sorrow. Breaking a cup : Death of an enemy. Having an elegant cup: Fortune in love affairs. Drinking from a gold cup: Advancement in own affairs. Receiving a cup as a gift: You have faithful friends.

CUPBOARD:

An empty cupboard : Business will not prosper. A full cupboard : Change for the better. Putting things in a cupboard: Will recover from loses. Taking out of a cupboard: You have many loyal friends.

CURSE:

Of cursing : Will have bad luck. Being cursed: Ambitions will be realized. Hearing curses: Difficulties have been surmounted. Hearing others curse you: Warning of love troubles.

CURTAIN:

Of many curtains: Own curiosity will bring damages. Pulling a curtain aside: Will be warned in time. Others pulling curtains aside: Warning of trouble. Putting up new curtains: Will entertain a prominent guest.

CUSHION:

Having a few cushions : Will make a good marriage. Having plenty of cushions: Difficulties and business worries. Cushiuons belonging to others: Discord among friends. Lying on several cushions: Change for the better.

CUT:

Being cut : Will be betrayed by a friend. A cut healing: Will have good earnings. A cut not healing: will be paid for your services. Treating a cut: Big joy. Children being cut: Approcahing money. Cutting off the head of a bird: Will have pleasures. Cutting off the head of animals: Joy. cutting off the head of another person: Revenge will be sought. Cutting stones: Profit. Cutting grass and shrubs: Fortune in business. Cutting with a saw or file: Unpleasant events are ahead. Being a cutter: infidelity.

CYCLING:

Of cycling : Will make a visit at some distance place.

Others cycling: Luck and prosperity. Relatives cycling: Misfortune in love affairs. Children cycling: Abundant means.

CYCLONE:

Of a cyclone : Intense sorrow will come to you. Being in the area of a cyclone: Warning of troubles. Prosperty being damaged by a cyclone. Social activities of a happy nature. Ships at sea being damaged by a cyclone: Death of an enemy.

D

DAFFODILS:

Of daffodils : Happiness in love affairs. Daffodils growing out of doors: Will have a long happy future. Receiving daffodils as a gift: Happiness is assured.

DAGGER:

Of a dagger : Expect news from an absent person. Many daggers: Beware of treachery. Others with daggers: Happiness is assured. Carrying a dagger: Advancement in own position. Attacking someone with a dagger: Own plans will be realized. Being wounded by a dagger: another person. is enjoying what you hoped for.

DAIRY:

Of a dairy : Good luck. Buying produce from a dairy: A change for the better. Working at a dairy: Failure of enemies.

DAISIES:

Of daisies in a garden : You are headed for success. Picking daisies: Great happiness in love. Having them in a vase in the home : Important and very beneficial events.

DANGER:

Being in danger : Success and honor. Facing danger: You may expect success. Avoiding danger: Teoubles will come to you. A lover being in danger: Failure. A married person being in danger: Disaster is ahead.

DARK:

Being in the dark: Difficulties ahead. Failing and hurting yourself in the dark: Expect changes for the worse. Succeeding in groping way out to the light: Big success. Others being in the dark : Loneliness and trouble. Children being in the dark: Illness. Walking in the dark: Recovery of money.

DAUGHTER:

A parent dreaming of a daughter : pleasure and harmony in the home. Own daughter playing: Happiness is assured. Several daughters gathered together: Advancement in own position. Talking to a daughter: Will have emotional sorrow. A mother dreaming of her only daughter: Will become pregnant soon. An adopted daughter: Serious disaster ahead.

DAWN:

A very clear dawn : Will receive unexpected help. A cloudy dawn: Death of an enemy. A rainy dawn: Good times are coming.

DEAF:

Being deaf : A big fortune is coming to you. other people who are deaf: Change for the better. Going deaf very suddenly: Advancement in own position.

DEATH:

The death of a pregnant woman: Will receive a fortune from abroad. The death of a young girl or boy: Will have a big happy family event. The death of a wife: Seperation from friends. The death of a husband: Death of a relative. Wanting death: Will have good health for a long time. Someone coming to life after death: High honor. The death of several people: Big happiness.

DEBTS:

Payment debts : Important and very beneficial event to come. Owing debts to other people: You are goodhearted. Others repaying debts owed you: Expect a loss. Having no intention of paying debts: Catastrophe ahead.

DECORATE:

Decorating own room : Losses in business affairs. Decorating a house: Loss of friend. Decorating a window : Take advantage of opportunities. Decorating a show window: Change for the better. Decorating a grave: Will have very little joy.

DEEDS:

Signing a deed: You are in danger. Having already signed a deed: Loss of money. Others signing a deed to you: Loss of affection. Receiving payment of a deed: Will have good health until death.

DELICATE:

Having delicate health: Change for the better. Others having delicate health: Will be vigrous in business activity. Children habing delicate health: Avoid rivals. Relatives having delicate health: Warning of troubles.

DELIGHT:

Being delighted : Exessive happiness. Others being delighted: Expect troubles at home and business worries. Relative being delighted: Triumph over enemies. Children being delighted: Financial gains.

DEMOLISH:

Of demolishing : People are talking against you. A house being demolished: Will have successful ventures. A building being demolished: Will be accused of wrongdoings. People demolishing machinery: Will receive money soon.

DENTIST:

Being in a dentist's chair : Will have cause to question friends's sincerity. Others in a dentist's chair: Business partners are not sincere. Children in a dentist's chair: Will hear false reports about friends. Friends in a dentist's chair: Misfortune in love affairs.

DEPART:

Of departing : Will barely avoid an unhappy event. Departing for a place of pleasure: Danger of losing property. Loved ones departing: Failure of projects. Departing with others: Death of an enemy. Others departing unwillingly: Unhapiness or death.

DESK:

Working at a desk : Bad luck: Working on an open desk: expect good news. A closed desk: Will have emotional sorrow. Others working at several desks: A mystery will be solved. Working on a desk at home: Happiness is assured. Working at a lawyer's desk: Advancement in own position. Working at an accountant's desk: Overwork on scientific matters.

DESPAIR:

Of despair : Luck and prosperity. Being in despair:

Domestic happiness. Not being in despair: Abundant means. Others being in despair: Will have a change for the better.

DEW:

Seeing the dew at dawn : You have one loyal friend. Refreshing dew falling: Abundant means. Dew on dead bodies: Big joy.

DIAMONDS:

Of diamonds : Failure in own personal matters. Having diamonds: Fortunate dealing in business and speculations. LOsing diamonds: Poverty and ill health. Finding diamonds: You have a good lover. Owning many diamonds: Success and honor will be conferred upon you. Others wearing diamonds: Will make a big profit. Buying diamonds: Will have emotional sorrow. Selling diamonds: Serious disaster ahead. Stealing diamonds: Will have big business losses. Of fake diamonds: Death of an enemy.

DICE:

Playing with dice : Fortune will change. Winning while playing with dice: Will receive an inheritance. Losing while playing with dice: Losses through speculation. Others winning while playing with dice: Recovery from lose of money. Others cheating while playing with dice: Abundant means.

DIET:

Of dieting : Dissolution of hopes. Being weak from dieting: Loss of wealth. Dieting too much: Danger of sickness. Others who are dieting : You have a kind heart. Friends disting: Will have a law suit.

DIFFICULTY:

Being in great difficulty of any kind: Change for the better. Having personal difficulties: Good times are coming. Having financial difficulties: Will receive money. Having dangerous difficulties in own life: Big happiness. Sweetheart having difficulties: Will surely be kind and agreeble. Others having difficulty: All will be well. Relatives having difficulty: Happiness is assured.

DINNER:

Having dinner : Warning of trouble. Having friends for dinner: Triumph over enemies. Having relatives for dinner: Must control your nerves. Having dinner with a large group: Will enjoy companionship of friends. Others giving a dinner party: You have one loyal friend.

DISASTER:

Being in a disaster : Will have good earnings. Others being in a disaster: Avoid rivals. A woman dreaming of a disaster: Suitable time to pursue endeavoes. A man dreaming of a disaster: Good times are coming.

DISEASE:

Having a disease : Warning of treachery. Others having a disease: Will make money illegally. Lovers dreaming of a disease: Good times are coming. Having a diseas in the stomach: Waste of money. Having a disease in the brain: Will be fortuneate and honored. Having an unknown diseas: Big financial gain.

DISH:

Breaking dishes : Domestic troubles. Others breaking dishes: Must control your passions. Chipping a baked enamel dish: Will receive plenty of money. Dropping a plate belonging to a scale: Big fortune in ahead.

DISINHERIT:

Being disinherited : Will sustain a serious loss. Disinheriting a relative: Will have good earnings. Others being disinherited: Change in your environment.

DISLIKE:

Disliking someone : Will have emotional sorrow. Someone disliking you: Will have worries. Being disliked by others without caring: Will have abundant means. Others disliking you: Difficulties will be overcome. Being disliked by member of the family: Happiness is assured.

DISMISS:

Having been dismissed from business position : Advancement in position. Dismissing an employee: Doomed for disappointment. Other being dismissed: A mystery will be solved.

DISPUTE:

Having a dispute: Will have a happy life. Having a dispute with relatives: Obstacles will be avoided. Having a business dispute: Discovery of lost valuables. Others having a dispute: Good times are coming.

DESTRESS:

Being in distress: Will have family quarrels. Children being in distress: Warning of trouble. Wife or husband being in distress: Will have emotional sorrow. Others being in distress: Will have big gains in fortune. Putting others in distress: Warning of trouble.

DISTURB:

Being distrubed: Will receive news from faraway. Others who are disturbed: Happiness is assured. Being disturbed by others: Persecution from an enemy.

DIVORCE:

Wanting a divorce : Domestic happiness. Being divorced: Security. Obtaining a divorce and receiving alimony: Prosperity. Relatives being divorced: Bak gossip by friends.

Doctor:

Going to a doctor: Will have mastery over many things. Calling a doctor for yourself: Will live a long life. Calling a doctor for children: New interests and surroundings. Calling a doctor for relatives: RApid recovery. CAlling a doctor for friends: Suitable time to pursue endeavors. A doctor visiting patients: Big wealth. Others calling a doctor: Troubles ahead: Being a doctor: Joy and profit. Becoming a doctor: Financial gains.

DOUBT:

Being in doubt : It is safe to rely on a good friend. Others doubting you: You distrust your friends. Being doubted by lover: Good luck. A wife doubting her husband: A long happy future. A husband doubting his wife: Happiness is assured.

DOWRY:

A woman giving a dowry to her husband: People will take good care of you. A man giving property to his bride: Expect much uneasiness. Giving a dowry to daughters: Will earn more money. A widow's dowry: Will make a good change in your life.

DRAWERS:

Of an open drawer : Suitable time to pursue flirtations. Opening a drawer: Hapiness is assured. Opening a locked drawer: Will discover a secret. Being unable to open a closed drawer: Beware of troubles ahead. A married woman dreaming of her drawers: Unfaithful to the man who loves her. A married man dreaming of his drawers: Shame and sorrow. A single girl dreaming of her drawers: Will soone be engaged. A single man dreaming of his drawers: Will be engaged to a rich girl soon.

DREAM:

Consulting someone about your dreams : Expect news from faraway. Dreaming nice things: You have impossible desires. Dreaming of being rich: Will be disillusioned. Dreaming of being poor: Change in your position. Others dreaming: Will have emotional sorrow.

DRIVING:

Of driving: Discovery of lost valueables. Other people driving: Expect monetary losses. Relatives driving: Listen to suggestions of friends. Loved one driving: Avoid rivals.

DROWN:

Of drowning: Will lose all that you have. Relatives drowning: Big ruin ahead. Being rescued from drowning: Expect help from a friend. A businessman drowning: Will go into bankruptcy. Other people drowning: Joy and triumph. Being drowned by others: Loss of money. Drowning own children: Will have an unhappy trip. Husband or wife drowning: Serious disaster is ahead. Rescuing others from drowning: A friend will reach a high position. Children being recued from drowning: Will have prosperity and high position.

DUMB:

Being dumb: Will have a family quarrel. Being unable to speak: Avoid speculation. Members of family being dumb: A crippled child will be born. Other people being dumb: Do not discuss your business plans.

DYE:

Dyeing own hair: Warning of trouble. Dyeing another's hair: Joy without profit. Others dyeing their hair: Will suffer through own foolishness. Putting rouge on cheeks: Will live a long life. Dyeing materials: Misery. A person who dyes materials: Must endure a long infirmity. Dyeing clothes: Business is very confused. Dyeing with light colors: Sickness is forthcoming. Dyeing with yellow or dark colors: Family member will have a high fever. Making a mess while dyeing clothes: Expect a very expensive present.

DYING:

Of dying: Will receive empty promises. Relatives dying: will receive a big inheritance. Children dying: Will receive fortune from abroad. Kissing a dying person: Loss of a lawsuit. Friends dying: Triumph over enemies. Others are dying: Doomed for disappointment.

DYSENTERY:

Having dysentery: Will receive a very costly gift. Taking medicine for dysentery: A good future is ahead. Children having dysentery: Will be invited to a banquet. Recovering from dysentery: Will receive news of a marriage. Entire family having dysentery at the same time: Domestic troubles.

E

EAGLE:

An eagle flying: Good fortune is ahead. Killing an eagle: Wealth and nothing to prevent achieving goal. A dead eagle: Expect money losses. Being attacked by an eagle: Expect many difficulties. A wounded eagle: Loss in love affairs. An eagle high up on a status: Will realize high ambitions. An eagle perched on a mountaintop: Fame and money. CArrying an eagle: Shame and sorrow. A woman dreaming of several eagles: Will have a famous son. Owning an eagle: Honors and business profits. An eagle standing up: Many soldiers will die. An eagle falling on you: Warning of danger. A bald eagle: Will have a prominent political position.

EARRINGS:

Of own earrings: Congenial work and good news. Losing own earrings: A period of sorrow is about to come. Earrings of others: Big friendship. Wearing earrings: Will be cheated by friends. Giving own earrings to someone: Big quarrel. Receiving earrings as a gift: Avoid rivals.

EARTHQUAKE:

Feeling an earthquake: Death of a relative. Being in the area of an earthquake: Loss of a close friend. The earth trembling from an earthquake: Loss in business matters. A city destroyed by an earthquake: A change in life will soon come. Earthquake occurring in the east: Difficulties must be overcome. Earthquake occurring in the west: Warning of troubles. Earthquake occurring in the North: Change in environment. Earthquake occurring in the south: Will have emotional sorrow.

ESLIPSE:

`The eslipse of the sun: Will incur losses. The eclipse of the moon: Will have small misfortune. Watching the eclipse of the moon with the family: Happiness. Watching the eclipse of the moon with a loved one: You are deceived.

EGGS:

Fresh eggs: Good news. Many broken eggs: Will quarrel and have lawsuits. Eating eggs: Foretells an early marriage. Having very fresh eggs: Will receive money. Having old eggs: Unpleasant news. Broken eggshells: Loss of money. White eggs: Will receive some advantageous news. Having brown eggs: Will receive bad news. Having red eggs: Will be threatened by someone. Eggs of different colors: Great disappointment. Buying eggs: Infidelity by a loved one. Cooking eggs: Gossip by friends. Chickens laying eggs: Abundant means. The eggs of a fish: Will have hard times ahead. Making a mess with eggs: Will be persecuted. Beating eggs with an egg beater: Death of a relative. The empty shells eggs: Will be eating too much.

ELEPHANT:

Of an elephant: Fear and danger for rich people. A poor person dreaming of an elephant: Will have a good, new position. Feeding an elephant: An important person will be friend you. Getting on the back of an elephant: Good fortune. Many elephants: Prosperity. Others with elephants: Will receive assistance from a friend. Giving water to an elephant:

Will be of service to an influential person. An elephant at a circus: Danger of death for a relative. An elephant escaping from a circus: Family quarrels. An elephant being free: Will enjoy much independence in life.

EMBRACE:

Embracing relatives: Watch out for treachery. Embracing children: Big joy is ahead. Embracing a stranger: Will entertain an unwelcome quest. Being embraced by others: Financial gains. Being embraced by unknown person: Suitable time to pursue flirtations. Wife or sweetheart embracing someone else: Loneliness and trouble. Husband or boyfriend embracing others: Will have a long life.

EMBROIDERY:

Of embroidering: Will make the best of everything. Having embroidered on a dress: Honor and riches. Having embroidered linens: Joy and profits. Embroidering something for loved one: Will be accepted in society.

EMPLOYMENT:

Being unable to find employment: Misfortune in love affairs. Having good employment: Good times are coming. Finding employment for others: Much poverty is ahead. Being at employment office seeking a job: Change for the better.

EMPRESS:

Being an empress: Loss of your lover. Being presented before an empress: Loss of dignity. Being married to an empress: Happiness is assured.

EMPTY:

Home being empty: Big catastrophe is ahead. Having ar

empty barrel: Big poverty. Pouring from an empty jar: Unexpected gains.

ENEMY:

Meeting an enemy: Good fortune. Being in the company of someone disliked: Catastrophe is ahead. Speaking with an enemy: Be cautious in dealings. Being taken away by an enemy: Will be embarrassed by friends. Fighting with enemies: Will be deceived by friends. Hating an enemy: Loss of your fortune. Killing an enemy: Great joy and pleasures in life. Winning out over an enemy: Will succeed in a law suit.

ENGAGEMENT:

A young person dreaming of being engaged: Will not be very popular. A broken engagement: May have to endure disappointments. A social high-class engagement: Troubles are ahead. Engagement of others being broken: Will have emotional sorrow. Engaged person being strong or beautiful: Dishonesty. Engaged person being quiet or simple: Future will be good.

ENVELOPES:

Of an envelope: Will receive sad news. A closed envelope: Difficulties are ahead. Opening an envelope and removing the contents: Worry will be smoothed away. Putting a letter in an envelope: Discovery of lost valuables. Receiving an envelope with many letters: Big disappointment in love. Mailing an envelope: Luck and prosperity. Buying envelopes: Change for the better.

ESCAPE:

Escaping from confinement: A rapid raise in the commercial world. Escaping from accident or injury: Good

..ings will come during life. Escaping from difficulties: Success in personal affairs. Escaping from fire: Triumph. Escaping from drowning: Will have anxious moments but success will come. Escaping from a furious animal: Treachery is near at hand. Being unable to escape: Honor and joy. Relatives escaping from danger: Financial gains. Others escaping from danger: Will be cheated by friends.

EXAMINATION:

Having an examination: Are unfitted to fill your position. Passing an examination: Expect business worries. Answering all questions correctly: Financial gains. Not answering questions correctly: Congenial work and good news. Children passing an examination: Will realize high ambitions. Others passing an examination: Doomed for disappointment.

EXCHANGE:

Exchanging articles in a store: Discovery of lost valuables. Exchanging articles with another person: Expect business losses. Exchanging articles with family memebrs: Troubles and difficulty. Exchanging wives between relatives: Rapid success of own hopes. Exchanging a blonde for a brunette: Will be married again.

EXERCISE:

Of exercising: All will be well. Feeling tired from exercising: Beware of monetary losses. Enjoying vigorous exercise: You are being deceived. Exercising with members of the family: Fortune and joy. Wife and husband exercising: Persecution and· treacher. Others exercising: Failure of enemies.

EXPLOSION:

Of an explosion: Friends will disapprove of your actions. Being injured in an explosion: Must endure vexation. Face being scarred by an explosion: Will be unjustly accused. Being enveloped in flames after an esplosion: Friends trespass on rights. Others being in an explosion: Danger to a relative. Being quilty of causing an explosion: Friends will lose confidence in you.

EXTINGUISH:

Extinguishing a fire: Great danger is ahead. Extinguishing a flame: Will not have sufficient money. Extinguishing a light: Serious quarrels over love. Extinguishing a law suit: Will be persecuted by a woman.

EYES:

Of many eyes: Good results in business. Having beautiful eyes: Love and joy. Having blue eyes: Tremendous joy. Having black eyes: Misery. Having brown eyes: Happiness. Having green eyes: Unexpected big wealth. Having red eyes: Illness. Having hazel eyes: Gossip by friends. Having crossed eyes: Will be short of money. Having big eyes: Will receive a large inheritance. Having small eyes: You are deeply loved. Having green and blue eyes: Big financial gains. Having grim eyes: Good business. The eyes of a healthy person: Business success. The eyes of a sick person: Will have a long life. Eyes being wide-open: A change in life will soon come. Having good eyeslght: Good health. Losing your eyesight: Children are in danger of death. Children's eyes: Financial gains. Admiring the eyes of your wife: You are unfaithful to your wife. Admiring the eyes of your husband: May expect a baby. Being worried about the eyes: Be careful of your actions. Being worried about children's eyes: Someone is working secretly against you.

EYEGLASS:

Wearing an eyeglass : Will fall into disgrace. Others people wearing eyeglasses : Good news will be received from a friend. Enemies wearing eyeglasses: A change in life will soon come.

F

FACE:

Seeing own fac in a mirror : Will not succeed in own plans. A beautiful face : Quarrels among lovers. A bright happy face : Good luck is ahead. An ugly face : Unhappiness in love affairs. A smiling face : Financial gains. A repulsive face : Failure of enimies. Childrens faces : Postponement of sucess. Faces of absolute strangers : Change of residence.

FAILURE:

Being a failure : Will relize high ambitins. Relatives being a failure : Use caution in business ventures. Others being a failure : Postponement of sucess. Husband being a failure : Are unfitted to fill your position.

FAINT:

Having fainted : Foretells illness. Suffering injury from fainting : Rapid success of own hopes. A member of the family fainting : A false friends is nearby. Children fainting : Unhappiness in love affairs. Others poeple fainting : Postponement of success.

FALL:

Failling from a high place : Misfortune is ahead. Falling from a medium high ; Loss f honor. Being injured in a fall : Will endure hardship and lose friends. Falling and being frightened ; Will experience some troubles. Falling without injury ; Will be victoriour in your struggles. Falling from a bridge : Madness. Falling and arising again : Honor. Falling in a grave hole: A catastrophe is ahead. Falling in the water : Risk of death for the dreamer. Falling in the ocean : Will have bad health. Falling in the ocean and then awaking with a start : Honor and wealth. Beibg thrown in the ocean by enemies : Will be persecuted. Others falling : Will be promoted. Relatives falling : Triumph over ememies. Children falling : Joy without profit. Enemies falling : Do not confide your secret. Friends falling : You are being deceived.

FAME:

Having fame : Will have dealings with authorities. Someone else achieving fame : Fame will be rich through own wo;rk. Children achieving fame : will live a long life. Mate achieving fame ; Failure of enemies.

FAMILY:

Of own family ; Be coutious in your ventures. Having a large family :Prosperous times are in store. Having a small family : A friend is trying to help. Having no family or relatives : You are being deceived. The family of other people : Failure of enemies.

FAREWELL:

Bidding farewell to someone else : Be cautions in business ventures. Bidding farewell to relatives : Will receive painful news. Bidding farewell to children : Worry will be smoothed away. Others bidding you farewell : Must control passions. Husband and wife bidding farewell ; A false is nearby.

FASTING:

Of fasting : Big honor. Members of family fasting with you : Big wealth. Fasting according to own religion : Happiness is assured.

FAT:

A woman dreaming of getting fat : She will be abandoned by her lover. A young girl dreaminf of grewing fat : Will be married soon. A man dreaming of growing fat : Will soon be a free man. A married woman dreading of growing fat : Happy days are ahead for her. A woman dreaming of getting really fat : Big wealth and honest love. Children getting fat : Wealth . Others women being fat: Dishonest and dangerour activities. Others women being fat : Dishonest and dangerous activities. Other people who are fast : Postponement of success. Eating fat : Success in love affairs. Cooking with fat : Good business ventures.

FATHER:

Of own father : Happines. Father being in a happy mood : Loss in business. Father dead : A big catastrophe is ahead. Father being poor : All desires will be accomplished. Own father passing away : Will not have success in business. Talking to your father : Virtue. The father of other people : A false frind is nearby.

FATHER IN LAW;

Of own father-in-law ; Important and very beneficial event to come. Father-in-law being dead : Will be threatened by people. Father-in-law being alive : Bad luck. Others father-in-law : Will be defficult to escape approaching troubles.

FEAR:

Having fear o;f something : Someone will take care of you. Overcoming own fears : Everything will go well. Having persisting fears : Will meet with deceit and treachery. Not knowing reason for fear; Do not trust one you now trust. Having great fears : You are a person of extraordinary courage.

FEATHER:

White feathers : Will be very lucky. Black feathers : Will be very unlucky. Red feathers :Gray feathers; Wealth. Light-blue feathers : realization of own ambitions. Ten feathers : Prospect of a journey. People wearing feathers in hats : Rapid success of own hopes. Collecting feathers : Will have joy during life. Wearing a tuft of feathers : Great honors will come to you.

FESTIVAL:

Of a festival : Expect difficulties in the near future. Preparing a festival : Another person is enjoying what you desired. Others at a festival : Joy and contentment. Being at a festival with relatives : Will receive happy news. Being at a festival with children : Happiness. Enemies being at a festival : Misery is ahead.

FEVER:

Having a very high fever : Friends will tell you lives. Suffering from a fever : Will be bothered by petty worries. Children fever : Financial gains. Friends having a fever : Will be cheated by friends.

FIGHT:

Of being in a fight : Misfortune in love affairs. Others

being in a fight : Recovery from a illness. Being beten in geght : Will have opposition in love. Winning a fight Will overcome your difficulties.

FILL:

Of filling : Will be involved in a secret transaction Filling bottles : Happiness for the woman of the house. Filling pockets : Honor. Filling a handbag : Will receive a gift of jewelry. Filling a hole : You enjoy amusements too much of the time.

FIRE:

Poking up a fire in a fireplace : You have no control of your temper. A blazing fire : Great joy will come to you. Lots of smoke but no flames : Will be disappointed. Being unaware of the fire : You are loved very much. Firemen putting out a fire : Will receive good news. A burning fire without smoke : Will have plenty of money. Someone falling fire without smoke : Will have plenty of money. Someone falling into a fire : Misfortune. Relatives burning in a fire : Will soon have a high fever. Watching a fire being put out : Being in a fire : Triumph. A dead fire : Will have bad fortune. A small fire ; Expect good news. A large fire : EXpect serour changes in your affairs. A big fire burning : Will soon have a quarrel. Being burned in a fire : Business damaged. Throwing water on a fire : Will lose you temper. Fire falling from the sky : Desolation. Starting a fire : Will allow yourself to be seduced. An artificial fire ; Will become pregnand soon. Taking something from a fire with hand : Will surmount obstacles. Extinguishing a fire completely : Will be compensated.

FISH:

Fish swimming freely about : Good fortune. Catching

fish : You will be loved very much. Dead fish in a store : Expect troubles. Fish in shallown water : Loss of reputation. A fish market : Will obtain a high honourable position. A woman dreaming of fishes of many colors : Illness. A man dreaming of fishes of many colors : Will quarrel and suffer. Having fish Will enjoy pleasures that will cost money. Cooking fish : Marriage. Eating boiled fish : Joy. Eating fried fish : Big worries. A dead fish in a stream : Loss of hope. Fish hatching : Will have difficulties in bearing a child. Catching a large fish : Joy and profit. Catching a small fish : Ruin in proportion to size of fish. Red-colore fish : Big contentment. Salted fish : Will have plenty to fight to avoid misery. Salmon fish : Dissatisfaction. Other people fishing : Will have children with poor health. Children fishing : Joy and health. Relatives fishing : Difficult business enterprises. Eating cod fish : Will receive good news. Buying cod fish ; Will have an unexpected visitor.

FLAG:

Carrying a flag : Honor will come to you. A flag floating in te breeze ; Will escape from threatened misfortune. Viewing a display of flags : Triumph over enemies. White flags : Success in own undertakings. Navy-blue flags : Promotion within employment. Yellow flag : Important changes in your affairs. Red flag : Warning of quarrels with friends. Will be unfortunate. Brown flag : Big frindship. Gold flag : Will do business with people fareway.

FLOAT:

Of something floating : All will go well. Having trouble staying afloat : Expect troubles ahead. Others floating : A false friends is nearby. A dead person floating near a beach : Will live a long life. A deal fish floating near the beach :

Danger though a secret. Am empty boat floting : Will have a change in surroundings.

FLOOD:

Of a big flood : Will be jilted by lover. Saving yourself from a flood : You have one loyal friend. Relatives being in a flood : A false friend is nearby. Others being in a flood : Will be unfortunate in love affairs. Flood causing devastation : Worry will be smoothed away. The ruin caused by flood : Postponement of success.

FLOWER:

Of flowers : Great happiness. Blooming flowers : Pleasures are ahead. A young woman dreaming of receiving flowers : Will have many suitors. Gathering flowers : Will marry soon. Receiving flowers a plant : Big benefit. A florist's yard full of flowers ; Will have big losses. Painted flowers : Will be worried. Artificial flowers : Misfortune in business. Receiving flowers as a gift : Big jou. Being greeted with flowers ; Pleasrure and contentment. Flowers blooming in May : Will have a better future. Own preferred flower : Will be blessed. White flowers ; Small difficulties . Yellow flowers : Big difficulties Red flowers : Death. Pink flowers : You are in love. Bright-colored flowers : Gloom is in store. Flowers of various other colors : Financial gains. Having flowers out of season : Obstacles are ahead. Flowers in the house : Pleasure and joy . Plants of flowers : Will have plenty of money. Pickling flowers : Will have a steady friendships : A yard full of flowers : Willhave weakness in your body. Smelling the scent of flowers coming from the yard : Loss of friends. Throwint flowers away : Violent quarrels. Throwing away blossoming flowers : Will suffer from own carelessness.

FLYING:

Of flying : Congenial work and good news. Flying at a high altitude : Big fortune. Flying at a low altitude : Ruin is ahead for you. A plane flying in distress : Loss through investments. Being an aviator : Ambitions plans are possibly beyond power to accomplish. Flying in a plane : Profitable speculation. Others flying : Be on the lookout for treachery. Owning a plane : Success in all enterprises.

FOREIGH COUNTRY:

Of a foreign country : Will be deceived. Going to foreign country : Your happiness lies at home. Being in a foreingn country alone : A change in life will soon come. Being in a foreign country with others ; Will have new business ventures. Being in a foreign country with a lady : Will be guilty of foolish actions. Being in a foreign country with a man : Must control passions. Being in a foreign country with loved one : Luck and prosperity.

FOREST:

Of a dense forest : Someone will care a lot for you. Being along in forest : Social activities of a happy nature. Being with others in a forest : Will be cheated by friends. A forest fire : Glad news. Wandering around in a forest : Inheritance. Relatives being in a forest : Will be jilted by your lover. Strolling though a forest : Pain is head for you. A forest with unusually high trees : Good business affairs.

FORTUNE:

Having own fortune told : Great struggle in real life. Reading fortune on a spinning a wheel : Beware of danger. Receiving fortune : Trouble and losses. Receiving a fortune from relatives : Success in everything. Being fortunate in business : Gay occasion to come. Being fortunate in love : Will lose plenty of money though gambling. Being fortunate in politics : Will have a steady position.

FOUNTAIN:

Of a sacred fountain : Devotion wıth bring success. A full fountain,: Happiness and long life. A fountain with high sprays : An unusually good thing will happen soon. Being at a fountain of clear water : Will be very happy in love . A large fountain ; Abundance and health. A fountain water : Profitable operation in business matters. Being at a fountain with sweetheart : Great happiness & success in love and marriage. A fountain with muddy water : Good luck to come later. A fountain with littered water : Troubles and vexation. Washing yourself at a foutain : Joy and prosperity. Drying yourself at a fountain : Poverty or death. A dry fountain : Big desolation.

FRAGRANCE:

A pleasant frangrances : Important and very beneficial event to come. An employment fragrance : Bad results, not too serious. A preferred fragrance : Small success.

FRIENDS:

Friends being happy ; Pleasant tidings. Friends being thoubled : Sickness is near at hand. Saying good-by to a friend : Painful experinece ahead. Arguing with a friend : Joy. Being separated from a friend : Friends are endeavoring to destroy you.

Friends being in trouble will receive unexpected good news. A friend being naked : Will have a big fight. Embracing a friend : Treason. Talking with a friend in a room : Joy and consolation. Loughing with friends : Will dissólve your partnership. Making new friends : Will be in mourning soo.

FRYING:

frying food : Will be taken care of during old age. Frying food for a party ; Will have an unfortunate quarrel. Flying eggs : Will have financial gains. Frying chicken will live a long life. Frying potatoes will be loved dearly by someone new.

FUNERAL:

Being present at a funers : Will be lucky in love affairs. Going to a funeral with a loved one : You are envied by enemies Going to funeral with other people : Good health. Going to a funeral with family : Loss of friends. Being a pallbearer at a funeral : Will do something foolish. Attending funeral of best husband or wife. A woman attending a funeral in mourning : Unhappy married life.

FURNITURE:

Beautiful furniture : Abundant means. Common furniture : Will be a person of the working class. A wealthy woman having nice furniture : She will do something foolish. A common person dreaming of nice furniture : Much love. A business girl dreaming of having furnitures ; Will earn own living.

G

GAIN:

Making a big gain : Misfortune in love affairs. A successful business gain : A big catastrophe is ahead. Making a gain by cheating ; Shame and sorrow. Making a real-estate gain : Will have good friendship. Making a gain under unfair advantages : Recovery from an illness.

GAME:

Taking part in a game : Financial gains. Others playing a game : Worry will be smoothed away. Winding while playing a game : Misfortune in business. Your side winning a game : Loneliness and trouble. Your side losing a game : Important and very beneficial event to come. Children playing games : Fortune in own affairs.

GARLAND:

Of a garland :Financial gains. Having a garland of flowerst : You are in love. Receiving a gift of a garland of flowers : Luck and prosperity. Sending a gift of a garland of flowers : Be careful of rivals.

GAS:

Lighting a gas flame : Will find away to avoid threatened misfortune. Blowing out gas flame : Enemies are seeking to injure you. A gaslight being poor : Your interests will suffer.

GATE:

Of a gate : You are very much in love. Passing through a gate. Will be shocked with receipt of bad news. A broken gate : Misfortune. A closed gate : Will be appressed with insurmoutable difficulties. Locking a gate : Success in business. Other people being at your gate : Locking a gate sucess in business. Other people being at your gate : Friends are being untrue to you. The gate of others : Will be cheated by friends.

GEMS:

Of gems : Happiness through love. Buying gems : Fortunate business transactions. Selling gems : Misfortune in love affairs. Putting gems around the neck : Financial gains. Other people wearing gems : Discovery of lost valuables. Receiving a gift of a fem : Danger through a secret. Relatives having gems : Sickness within the family.

GHOST:

Of a ghost appearing : Good luck. Being frightened by a ghost : Expect troubles ahead. Having no fear of ghosts : Will pull through difficulties. A ghost speaking to you : Beware of enemies.

GIFT:

Receiving a gift : Will have riches and receives a marriage proposal. Receiving a gift from a loved one : Success and good luck. Giving a gift : Bad luck. Receiving several gifts : Beware of person from whom you receive them. Giving a gift to relatives : Good hopes. Receiving a gift from an important person will receive many honors. Receiving gifts from relatives : Postponement of success.

GIRL:

A beautiful girl : Increase in business affairs. An intelligent girl : Big fortune. Talking to a girl : Happiness and tranquility. A single man dreaming of kissing a girl : Good luck. A married person dreaming person of kissing a girl : Domestic troubles. Kissing several girls running : Will catch a thief. A girl carying : Will be embarrassed by a friend. An exceptionally beautiful girl : Abundant means. Saving a girl from danger : Will be extremely loved. A kind girl : Happiness in love affairs. Receving suprising news from a girl : A long-delayed reply with arrive. A man dreaming of being a girl ; Will play a female part on stage.

GOAT:

Reaching a goal in life ; Financial gains. Not reaching a goal in life : Luck and prosperity. Others reaching their goal in life : Important and very beneficial event. Making a goal while playing a game : Failure of enemies . OThers making a goal in a game : Will have a long life.

GOD:

Praying to God :Much prosperity. Workshiping God : Sickness. Hearing God speak to you : Intense enjoyment. Talking to God : Joy and happiness. God putting his arms around you : Will receive that prayed for. Seeing God face to face : Will have much joy. God granting you what was desired : Will rcalize high ambitions.

GOLD:

Finding gold : An inheritance will soon be yours. Seeing gold : Every enterprise will bring success. Losing gold : Financial distress. Digging for gold : unexpected fortune will come through own efforts. Working this gold misfortune. Clothes being embroidered with gold : You are highly through of by others. Making rings from gold : Loss of time. Imitation gold : You will be plenty rich.Exchanging gold : will lose your temper. Throwing gold away : Big sorrow. Handling gold in a business venture :You are a tempermental person. MElting gold : Someone is doing you wrong. Talking gold from others : Big fortune. Stealing gold : You will get into troubles. Counting gold and silver : Will have a large loss. The color of gold will do business with people faraway. Masterials of any kind in gold color : Abundant means. Buying clothes of gold color : Approaching money. Gold planing ; Will receive high honors.

GOOD:

Of good things : Misfortune in love. Doing good to others : Joy and pleasure. OThers doing good to you : Profit and gains. Children doing good things : A baby will be born late in life. Saying good things about others : Will be embrassed. People saying good things about you will be deceived by friends.

GOWN:

Wearing a beautiful gown : Misfortune in love affairs. Own gown being shabby : Advancement within own position. Own gown being town : Luck and prosperity. Gown being pulled away and being left naked : Abundant means.

GRAVE:

A newly prepared grave : Will suffer through the sins of others. Walking on a grave : Unhappy married life. Of own grave

Enemies are trying to bring disaster to you. Digging a grave :

Big

obstacles are head. Walking an other person's grave : Death is very near at hand. Grave space being open : Will receive news from afar. The grave of your father : Inheritance. Building a grave ; Loss of friends. Destroying a grave : A wedding will take place soon.

GRIEF:

Of suffering grief : You will be happy soon. Children suffering grief : Joy and merry times ahead, Relatives suffering grief : Something good will happen to loved one. Enemies suffering grief : Unhappiness.

GROOM:

Of a groom : Hard work awaits. Being a groom : Legal affairs will be made known to you. Several grooms : Will have to countend with fuffians. The groom of an enemy : Thing will go as planned .

GUN:

Having a gun : Danger is head. Receiving a gun as gift Honor. Buying a gun. Good earnings. Hearing a gun fired : Loss of employment. Shooting a person with a gun Big dishonor. Being shot by a gun : A serious illness threatens. Heaving shot someone with a gun : A loved one will pass away. Others firing a gun : Will be an invalid for some time. Shooting an enemy with gun : Will have a laaw suit. A rifle with a bayonet ; Seperation of partners. Travelling with a gun : Will soon get married. A gun merchant : Will dissolve a corporation.

H

HABIT:

Having good habit : Will receive good news. Having bad habits : Sickness. Having a special habit : Will be welcomedd wherever you go. Relatives having good habits ; Will be humiliated Others having bad habits ; Will be humiliated others having bad habits : Warning of troubles.

HAIRPIN:

Of hairpins : You hairpins : You are being deceived. Handling hairpins : Will visit a novel place of amusement. Finding others hairpins on the floor : A friend is watching you. Buying hairpins : Approching money. Losing hairpins : A change will come soon. Finding hairpins of a vival woman : Will be guilty of foolish actions.

HALL:

Being in a hall : A two-faced companion will injure your reputation. Being in a hall with others : Will receive bad news. Having a meeting in a hall with friends : Good, new relationships. Meeting in a hall with enemies : Advancement within own position.

HAMMER:

Having a hammer in own hands : Pleasant work and good news. Hammering on wood : Avoid rivals. Hammering on plaster : Will be jilted by a lover. Others holding a hammer

: Temptation will come to you. OThers hammering ; Financial condition will be better in the future. The sound of a hammer being used: You have one loyal friend. Hearing many people hammering : Happiness in love affairs.

HAND:

Of own hands : Perfec accord between husband and wife. Having a big hand : Will be a big lover. Having a small hand :

Infidelity. Own hand being cut : Will incur debts. Burning own hand: Loss of employees. Hands being clean: Will overcome troubles. Hands being dirty: Be careful with own affairs. Shaking hands: Unexpected good events.

HANDKERCHIEF:

Losing a handkerchief: Broken engagement. A torn handkerchief: Serious troubles between lovers. Giving a handkerchief as a gift: Will cry for a long time. Using a handkerchief to blow nose: Will be loved by people. A linen handkerchief: Will soon become ill. A silk handkerchief: You are egotistical. An embroidered handkerchief: You are prone to conceit. Wiping sweat away with a handkerchief: Troubles are ahead. Putting a handkerchief: Be careful of new ventures. Receiving a handkerchief as a gift: Will receive a gift.

HAPPY:

Of being happy: Will realize your ambitions. Increased happiness: Bad business ventures according to degree of happiness. Husband and wife being happy: Joy and success. Children being happy: Rapid success of own hopes. Relatives being happy: Worry will be smoothed away. Friends being happy: A false friend is nearby. Other people being happy: Avoid rivals. Employees being happy: Pleasant social activities.

HARVEST:

Having a good harvest: Misfortune in love affairs. Workers barvesting: Money will come easily. Having an abundant harvest: Nature favours you. A poor harvest: Troubles in love affairs.

HATE:

Being hated without reason: Will possess many true friends. Hating others: Be careful not to do them wrong unconsciously. Hating enemies: Will win a lawsuit. Being hated by friends: Will have new, good friends. Hating some of own relatives: Happiness in domestic affairs.

HEAR:

Hearing someone nearby: Will have a vigorous mind: Hearing relatives talking: A change in life will soon come. Hearing children: Financial gains. Hearing others: You are being deceived.

HEARSE:

A hearse being at a church: Worry will be smoothed away. A hearse taling a dead person to the grave: Happiness. A military hearse conveying the dead: Will have emotional sorrow.

HELP:

Requiring help: Attempt to understand the heart of your acquaintances. Hiring help: Will have hard work ahead. Firing help: You expect too many favours of others. Having reliable help: Misery. Asking for financial help: Joy. Receiving help from a dog: Will be couble-crossed by a woman.

HIDE:

Of hiding: Bad news will soon reach you. Relatives hiding: You are being deceived. Others hiding: Avoid rivals.

HISTORY:

Of past history: Big honors. Reading a history book: Will go into bankruptcy. Being a history teacher: Security in business. Consulting a book on ancient history: Your fortune is at expense of others. Reading modern history books: Don't believe lies being told by others.

HOBBY:

Spending time at favourite hobby: Joy without profit. Others spending time at their hobby: A change in life will come. Children speinding time at their hobby: Financial gains.

HOLE:

Making a hole: Will make a long trip. Others making holes: Good times will come in the future. Falling into a hole: Illness. Creeping into a hole: Will come in contract with undesirable people.

HOME:

Of a home: Financial security. Own home: Happiness with in the family. Others peoples' homes: Will have a law suit coming up. Building a home: Honor without joy. Others buildinga home: Will have much consolation. Changing homes: Small fortune. Your home burning: Honour and dignity.

HONEY

Having honey: Business success. Eating honey: Big success in all own dealings. Being given honey: Financial gains. Making honey on a farm or in backyard: Big prosperity.

HONEYMOON:

Going on a honeymoon: Changes in your life will come. Being on own honeymoon: You are being deceived. Children going on their honeymoon: Joy without profit. Relatives going on their honeymoon: Will take a small trip. Friends going on their honeymoon: Disappointment.

HOROSCOPE:

Buying a horoscope book: Approaching money. Being told your horoscope: Will be badly tormented. Reading own horoscope: Will be embarrassed.

HOSPITAL:

Of a hospital: Misery. Being a patient in a hospital: Hopes for good business. Being in a religious hospital: Divine hopes. Being in a mental hospital: Must control passions.

HOUSE:

Of a house: Financial security. Own house: Happiness within the family. A house belonging to others: Will have a lawsuit coming up. Building a new house: Honor without joy. Changing houses: Small fortune. A house burning: Honour and dignity. Others building a house: Will have a big consolation. Friends visiting your house: Sorrow. A house being torn down: Warning of sad news.

HURT:

Being hurt: Will be plenty rich. Children being hurt: Financial gains. Relatives being hurt: You are being watched by one with evil entent. Enemies being hurt: Family quarrels.

HUSBAND:

Of a husband when not married: Bid joy. Having a good husband: Avoid rivals. Liking someone else's husband: Trouble is ahead. Wanting to divorce your husband: Must control your passions. Losing husband by death: Important and very beneficial events to come. Marrying a second husband: Luck and prosperity. A husband divorcing his wife: Quarrels with one dear to you. Other flirting with your husband: Will live together all your life.

I

ICE CREAM:

Eating ice cream: Success in every undertaking. Buying ice cream: Danger through a secret. Making ice cream: Financial gains. Children eating ice cream: Will live a long life. Enemies eating ice cream: They must endure starvation.

ILLNESS:

Having an illness: Misfortune in love affairs. Children having an illness: Consolation and happiness. Relatives having an illness: Unhappiness. Enemies having an illness: Great temptation will not be favourable for you. Visiting people with an illness: Will find a way to attain own goal. A woman dreaming of having an illness: Dispair. Sweetheart having an illness: Must forego some anticipated pleasure. Other people having an illness: Someone you know will go to prison. Many people in a hospital with illness: Joy and profit. Having a brain illness: Fortune. Having a stomach illness: You waste money. Having an unknown illness: Wealth.

INCOME:

Having a comfortable income: You should mend your ways in life. Having insufficient income: Warning of troubles with relatives. Own income getting very low: Important and very beneficial events to come. Relatives with a big income: Use caution in business ventures. Friends with a big income: A false friends is nearby.

INFANT:

A newborn infant: Pleasant surprises are awaiting. A helpless infant: Warning of coming trouble. A beautiful infant: Peace and joy. A newborn infant in diapers: Good events to come. An infant nursing: Long illness. A wetnurse nursing your infant: Beware of threats. The infant of another person: Unhappiness in love affairs.

INFLUENZA:

Having influenza: Fortune is ahead. Members of family having influenza: A secret will be discovered. Children having influenza: Will lead a simple and honest life. Dying from influenza: Faithful friends will show compassion toward you.

INHERITANCE:

Receiving an inheritance: Death in the family. Not receiving an inheritance: Death of a brother. Receiving a small inheritance: Affiction. Being cut off from an inheritance: Will fall into misery.

INNOCENT:

Being innocent: You are a very passionate person. Knowing that you are not innocent: Will acquire a new and important position. An innocent person being found guilty: Fortune is ahead. Members of family being innocent: Will have business arguments.

INSULT:

Insulting someone else: You have deceitful friends. Being insulted by others: A season of sorrow is coming. Being insulted by friends: Troubles are ahead. Insulting friends: Will suffer through own foolishness. Being insulted by enemies: Change of occupation. Insulting enemies: Luck and prosperity. Being insulted by relatives: Change of residence. Being insulted but not resenting it: Beware of troubles ahead.

INVENTOR:

Being an inventor: High honours. Other inventors: Will be compensated through their work. Children becoming inventors: Luck and prosperity.

IRONING:

Ironing clothes: Will experience trouble because of a rival. Ironing a man's clothes: Comfortable home and increasing love. Ironing dresses: Quarrels with husband. Ironing lines: Keep yourself free of any ties. Ironing silk materials: Unexpected help will come to you. Ironing starched clothes: Illness within the family.

IVORY:

Possessing ivory: Will have a literary talent. Buying ivory: You have one true and trusted friends. Selling ivory: Misery. Giving ivory as a present: Money will come easily during life.

J

JAIL:

Being in fall: Public esteem. Being in jail for a long time: Bad destiny. Being promptly released from jail: Use caution in business activities. Being in a dark jail: You have a secret friend. Being in jail for life: Will receive a big favour. Being in jail because of friend's wrongdoing: Sorrow. Friends being in jail: Family happiness. Enemies being in jail: Short-lived fortune. A woman dreaming of being in jail: Must endure much suffering.

JAM:

Making jam: Will have many charming friends. Buying jam: Will have a happy home. Giving children jam to eat: Family happiness. Receiving jam as a gift: Postponement of success.

JAR:

Of an empty jar: Will receive a letter from abroad. A full jar: Will have wealth late in life. A jar wich candy in it: Worry will be smoothed away. Breaking a jar: Rapid success of own hopes.

JEALOUS:

Being jealous: Prepare yourself for unpleasant news. Being jealous of husband: Be cautious in your ventures. Being jealous of wife: Pleasant social activities. Being jealous of children: Family quarrels. Being jealous of sweetheart: Important and very beneficial event to come. Being jealous of your religion: Hope in God.

JEWEL:

Having jewels: Unhappiness in love affairs. Buying jewels: Will have an accident. Wearing jewels: Will suffer because of envy. Steeling jewels: Are in danger of committing some disgraceful act. Receiving a gift of jewels: You are hated by someone. Admiring jewels: Will experience extravagance. Giving a gift of jewels: Will experience ruin. Selling jewels: Loss of money. Being a jeweler: Will cheat friends.

JOKE:

Telling a joke: Will enjoy good humor. Listening to good jokes: Extreme misery. Telling dirty jokes: Will make a big profit. Telling very funny jokes: Will endure affliction. Hearing children telling jokes: Unhappiness will be consoled.

JOURNEY:

Going on a journey: Profits if the fourney is pleasant. Going on a disagreeable journey: Big disappointment. Going on a journey on horseback: Will surmount your obstacles. Walking all the way on a journey: Hard work is ahead. Taking a journey in a carriage: Big fortune. Taking a journey in a car: Abundant means. Taking a journey by steamer: Accord among friends. Taking a journey by plane: Family quarrels. A long journey: You will be able to avoid unpleasant things. Going on a journey armed: Will soon get married. Going on a journey with a sword at your side: Will be married in a month. Taking a journey on a rough road: Everything will turn out well. Having stormy weather during a journey: Be careful in own affairs. Relatives taking a journey: Change for the better. Enemies taking a journey: Failure of enemies. Taking a journey with children: Happiness is assured.

JUNGLE:

Of a jungle: Financial affairs will cause anxiety. Being in a jungle: Economize while there is still time. Others being in a jungle: Discovery of lost valuables. Killing a wild animal in a jungle: You have several loyal friends.

K

KETTLE:

Of a kettle : Hard work awaits. A kettle of boiling water: Troubles will soon end. An empty kettle: A change awaits. A bright kettle that is very clean: Big losses in business.

KEYS:

Having a key: Will become very enreged. Having lover's keys: You will come out well from a present danger. Having a broken key: Illness. Finding several keys: Peace and happiness in the home. Losing own keys: Misfortune in love affairs. Giving keys to someone: Good fortune in home life.

KIDNAP:

Being kidnapped: Change in your environment. A girl being kidnapped: Misfortune in love matters. A boy being kidnapped: A catastrophe is ahead. Kidnappers being arrested: Approaching money.

KITS:

Making a kite: You will risk all through speculation. A kite flying easily in the breeze: Expect success. A kite flying low: Good times will come in the future. A kite flying very high: Big joy.

KNIFE:

Of a knife: Will be invited to a big dinner. A sharp knife: Many worries. A rusty knife: Discontent and vexations at home. A broken knife: Failure in love. A kitchen knife: Quarrels with friends. A butcher's knife: Good times are coming . Having many knives: Quarrels. A table knife: Will have a big argument. Having a pocketknife: Separation of lovers. Finding a knife: Failure in business. Cutting yourself with a knife: Must curb your emotions. Being wounded with a knife in the neck: Will be insulted by friends. Two knives in the position of a cross: Someone will be killed.

KNITTING:

Of knitting: Will have peace in the home. Doing fancy knitting: Will have a loving husband. A young woman knitting: Will make a hasty marriage. Mother knitting: Will have obedient children. Children knitting: Prosperity in the home. Enemies knitting: Undertakings will be crowned with success. Others knitting: You are being deceived by friends.

L

LADDER:

A tall ladder: Will be jilted by your sweetheart. Climbing a ladder: Unusual happiness and prosperity. Descending a ladder: Disappointments in business. Falling from a ladder: Failure. Climbing a circular ladder: Will attain own goal. Descending a circular ladder: Worry will be smoothed away. Being dizzy when on a ladder: Important and very beneficial event to come. Climbing a rope ladder: Profit. Carrying a ladder with you: Will rescue someone. Raising a ladder up to a windows: Will encounter a tender person. Climbing a ship's gangway: You will be robbed. Others climbing a ladder: You have faithful friends. Climbing a house ladder: Success. Climbing the ladder of a fortress: Advantageous lawsuit. Jumping from a ladder: Will obtain a good position. Climbing a stepladder: Unexpected good fortune.

LAMP:

Of a lamp: Business will come to a standstill. Lighting a lamp: Will have to offer explanation to people. A lighted lamp: Passion. A bright lamp: Good luck in a small venture. Turning out a lamp: Coolness in love. A very dim lamplight: Will work hard and face difficulties. Many lamps: Your path in life will be an easy one. A lamplight going out: Failure of your plans. A plain unlit lamp: You will fall in love. Lamps in the homes of others: Warning of trouble.

LANDSLIDE:

Of a landslide: Loneliness and trouble. Repairing a landslide: Discovery of lost valuables. Causing a landslide: Triumph over enemies.

LATE:

Being late: Your opinions will be sought. Being late to a meeting: Are confronted with insurmountable obstacles. Others being late: Loss of money. Friends being late: You are being deceived. Employees being late: Warning of troubles.

LAUGH:

Someone laughing: Be careful with love affairs. Several people laughing: Take precautions against gossipers. Being laughed at by a woman: She will deceive you. Children lauging: Approaching money. Enemies laughing: A rival is undermining your work. Hearing someone laugh: Indicates loss.

LAZY:

Being lazy: Trouble for those near you. A lazy couple: Legal matter will end in marriage. Husband being lazy: An unknown person is working against you. Wife being lazy: Dignity and distinction. Children being lazy: Will marry wealthy people. Employees being lazy: Worries will be smoothed away. Others being lazy: Warning of trouble.

LEATHER:

Of a leather shop: Failure of enemies. Buying leather: Happiness within the family. Working with leather: Financial gains. Selling leather products: Luck and prosperity. Giving a gift made of leather: Family quarrels. Receiving a leather purse as a gift: Doomed for disappointment. Having a harness, handbag, or belt of leather: Financial gains.

LEMON:

Of a lemon tree: You should mend your ways in life. An unripend lemon: Frivolity. A lemon blossom: Will take a trip abroad. Ripe lemons: Will fall in love. Eating lemons: Unhappiness. Drinking lemon juice: Good health. Eating sweet lemons: Prosperity. squeezing lemons: Will get rid of enemies. Drinking a hot lemonade: Improvement in health. Making medicine from sweet lemons: Will be good for your health.

LETTER:

Receiving a letter: Great wealth awaits. Receiving a letter from a wife or husband: Failure of enemies. Receiving a letter from a lover: Prompt engagement. Receiving a letter from a friend: Will have good earnings. Receiving a letter from children: Abundant means. Receiving a letter from relatives: Will come out well from a present peril. Receiving a letter from a suitor: Will make an advantageous marriage. Receiving a business letter: Be cautious in all your affairs. Receiving letters with money: Hopes have been accomplished. Having a letter of exchange: Unexpected profit. Writing letters to an attorney: Misfortune.

LIBRARY:

Of a library: Will make rapid progress. Owning a library: Will need to consult a judge. Borrowing a book from a library: Poverty. Consulting books at a liberary: You are prone to laziness.

LIGHTNING:

Of lightning: High honours. Lightning striking a house:

Death of a friend. Lightning striking trees: Discord between partners. Being struck by lightning: Death of a relative. Others being struck by lightning: Will meet a lustful woman. Lighting striking the water: Success is certain. Lightning killing animals in a field: Your life is in danger. Lightning striking at night: Troubles and quarrels.

LION:

Of a lion: Future dignity. A woman dreaming of hearing a lion roar: Unexpected promotion. A man dreaming of hearing a lion roar: Will be admired by woman. Being chased by a lion: Disgrace. Killing a lion: Financial independence. An angry lion: Expect misfortune caused by jealousy. The cub of a lion: Will have a valuable friendship.

LIPSTICK:

Wearing lipstick: You are surrounded by false friends. Other people wearing lipstick: Treason and false friendships. Buying lipstick: Frivolity. Catching a man with lipstick on his lips: Troubles from sweetheart or wife.

LOCK:

Of opening a lock: Happiness is assured. Being unable to open a lock: Beware of trouble ahead. A woman opening a lock: Will be unfaithful to the man who loves her. A man opening a lock: He is flirting with several woman. An opened lock: Suitable time to pursue your courtship. Being unable to find keys for a lock: Be careful in money matters. Finding the key for a lock: You will pull through your troubles. Having keys for locks: Avoid speculations of any kind. Possessing many locks: You have very stingy relatives.

LOOKING GLASS:

Of a looking glass: Treason: A woman looking at herself in a looking glass: Friends are cheating you. A man looking at himself in a looking glass: Be careful of business. A business executive looking into a mirror: Staff is not giving support. A young girl looking into a mirror: Advisable to change boyfriends. A married woman looking into a mirror: She is unfaithful to her husband. A lover looking into a mirror: Sweetheart is not really faithful. A widow looking into a mirror: Should find out the real underlying motive.

LOTTERY:

Of a lottery: You do not deserve success. Playing a lottery: Small risks are ahead. Being interested in a lottery: Unknown enemies are around you. Holding lottery tickets: Good luck. Lovers holding a lottery ticket: Unhappy association. A lottery drawing: You will make money. Lottery numbers being upside down: Engagement to a worthless person.

LOVE:

Being in love: Will live happily during life. Love being unwanted: Will have heart trouble. Being loved: Prosperity. Being in love with yourself: Vanity. Loving your work: Prosperity is ahead. Loving someone very much: Fortune and joy. Trying to make love to someone: Unhappiness. Not succeeding in love: Will marry and life happily. Being in the company of a liver: Will not succeed in marital life. Being in love with two people: Faith and confidence will be abused. Sweethearts being in love: Beware of jealous friends. Loving your children: Happiness. Being loved by children: Quarrels over which child is loved most. Loving your husband: Avoid rivals. Others loving your husband: Will live happily together all your live. Loving your wife: Luck and prosperity. Others loving your wife: Troubles are ahead. Loving your relatives: Loss of money. Being loved by relatives: Financial losses. Loving your friends: Will receive news of a friend's death. Being loved by friends: You will hear false promises.

LOVE LETTERS

Writing a love letter: Happiness. Reading a love letter: Will receive good news. Receiving many love letters: Frankness is an admirable quality. Tearing up love letters: Unhappiness. Saving treasured love letters: Will find out the truth.

LOVE TOKEN:

Giving a love token promise: Suitable time to pursue courtship. Receiving a love token promise: You are being deceived. Others knowing about a love token promise: Be cautious.

M

MAD:

Being insane: Happiness. A man dreaming of being mad: You love someone very deeply. A woman dreaming of being mad: Will have a son who becomes facous. A young girl dreaming of being mad: Will marry soon. Becoming mad: Long life. A raving mad person: Unhappiness is ahead. A mad person being dead: Will have a new love.

MAGNIFYING GLASS:

Of a magnifying glass: Business will be enlarged. Using a magnifying glass: Glorious future. Buying a magnifying glass: Discovery of lost valuables. Reading with a magnifying glass: Will live a short life.

MAIL:

Mailing a package: Will receive a gift. Mailing a letter with a ckeck: Will receive good news. Mailing documents: A false friend is cheating you. Mailing items of value: Will become jealous.

MAKE-UP:

A beautiful woman using make-up: Beware or you will be deceived. A plain woman using make-up: Will have troubles in love affairs. Being an arrogant, conceited woman and making-up: Danger of loss of estate. A man dreaming of a woman make-up: Loss of authority. A woman dreaming of using make-up: Satisfaction and good income. Putting a net over own hair: Will have a terrible headache.

MAP:

Of a colored map: Will have plenty of money. Studying a map: Change of residence. Consulting a man: Changes in business or employment. Buying a map: Will take a long trip abroad.

MARMALADE:

Making marmalade: Troubles and worries. Eating marmalade alone: Beware of untrue friends. Eating marmalade in company of others: Wealth. Giving marmalade as a gift: Good love affairs.

MARRIAGE

Of a marriage: Warning of ill health. Getting married: Melancholy. Assisting at a marriage: Will have pleasing news of little importance. A second marriage: Will make money. Giving sister away in marriage: Big peril. Children participating in a marriage: Good news. A woman dreaming of marriage to an old man: Sickness and trouble ahead. Giving a dauther away in marriage: Good times are ahead. A widower dreaming of marriage the second time: Happiness until death. Being a bridesmaid at a marriage: Will get married very soon. Being a flower girl at a marriage: Will have a happy future. The marriage of a priest: Success in life. Being a bride or groom: Profit. A young woman dreaming of being an unhappy bride: Enemies seek her downfall. A bride being with her parents: Danger. Being a beautiful bride: Joy. Being a plain bride: Advantages in life. Being an ugly bride: Unhappiness. Being a blond bride: Joy without profit. Being a brunette bride: Inheritance. Being a virgin bride: Big honor.

MATCHES:

Of matches: Own efforts will riches. Having a box of matches in pocket: Financial gains are at hand. Having matches at home: Misfortune in love affairs. Buying matches: Expect some money.

MEASLES:

Of having measles: Fretting and worry will interfere with own business. Other people with measles: Will be troubled over love affairs. Children having measles: Happiness is ahead. Relatives having measles: Approaching money.

MEDICINE:

Of a medicine chest: Big joy without profit. Taking medicine: Troubles are not serious: persevere, and you will succeed. Taking pleasant medicine: Troubles will end in ultimate good. Taking bitter medicine: Will attempt to injure one who trusts you. Giving medicine to friends: Accord among friends. Giving medicine to children: Hard work awaits. Giving medicine to relatives: Be cautious in all your dealings.

METALS:

Of metals: Riches. Buying metals: Approaching money. Selling metals: Abundant means. Melting metals: You are confronted with insurmountable obstacles.

MILK:

Of milk: Misfortune in love affairs. Drinking milk: Great joy. Selling milk: Fortune in love affairs. Spilling milk: Loss of business. A large container full of milk: Unexpected fortune. Milking a cow: Good times are coming. Getting lots of milk from a cow: Prosperity in love affairs. Having large quantities of milk: Good health. Giving milk to other people: Will lead a charitable life. Selling large amounts of milk: Abundant harvest for the farmer. A woman selling milk: Large profits for business people. A young girl milking a cow: Safe journey for the traveler. The milk of a donkey: Riches. The milk of a woman: Gossip. A married woman having plenty of milk: She will be pregnant again. An old woman having milk: Big wealth.

MIRROR:

Of a mirror: Discouragements. Seeing yourself in a mirror: Illness. Seeing husband in a mirror: Will be unfairly treated. Seeing a loved one in a mirror: Wealth. Seeing others in a mirror: Unhappy marriage. A broken mirror: Unexpected death of a relative. A woman looking at herself in a mirror: Friends are cheating you. A man looking at himself in a mirror: Be careful in own business. A young girl looking in a mirror: She should change boyfriends. A business executive looking in a mirror: Staff is not loyal to you. A widow looking in a mirror: Find out her ulerior motives.

MISTAKE:

Having made a mistake: Avoid conceit. Others making a mistake: Be sure of your information before acting. A wife and husband making a mistake: Take counsel before taking action. Making mistakes in accounts: What you desired will not be realized.

MONEY:

Possessing money: Great financial gains. Handling money: Will be deceived. Collecting money: Will have petty vexations. Paying money: Prosperity awaits you. Receiving money: Impending changes. Finding money: Danger and business loss. Losing money: Success. Counting money: Happiness. Assembling money: Will receive good news. Stealing money: Long sickness. Spending money: Will risk failure of plans. Changing paper money: Difficulties are your own fault. Changing gold money: Misfortune. Changing silver money: Will receive a visit from friends. Changing copper: Bad luck. Changing nickel: Obstacles are ahead. Handling foreign paper money: Financial losses. Handling foreign gold money: Beneficial gains. Handling stocks: Risk of failure. handling checks: Danger. Of a money changer: Will receive unpleasant news.

MONEY:

A full moon : Intense enjoyment of life. The moon shining brightly: Good luck. The moon being free of clouds: Success in love. The moon being clouded over: Interruption in comforts of life. A new moon: Will be very fortunate in business. A blood-red moon: Indicates strife. The reflection of the moon in water: Will fall in love with handsome man. The eslipse of the moon: Expect reverses in affairs. The moon falling from the sky: Loss of money. The moon moving toward the sun: Happiness. The moon at sunset: Death of a prominent person. Being illuminated by the moon: Will receive big favours from a woman. Going to the moon: Your desires are impossible. A woman dreaming of the moon getting bright: Big profit. A man dreaming of the moon getting bright: Honour and joy. A woman dreaming of the moon becoming dark: Loss of money. A man dreaming of the moon becoming dark: Unhappiness. A woman dreaming of a dark moon: Illness of the mother, sister or daughter. A man dreaming of a dark moon: Illness of the brain or eyes. A young woman dreaming of a dark moon: Will make a long trip.

MULTIPLY:

Multiplying figures: Don't trust acquaintances. Others multiplying figures: You are being deceived. Various things multiplying Watch enemies closely. Plants multiplying: Someone is endeavouring to destroy you.

MURDER:

Of a murder: Triumph over enemies. Murdering someone: Sorrow and failure. Others committing a murder: Will live a long life. Committing a murder: Disgrace through some dishonourable act. A murderer being arrested: A change in life will come soon. Being murdered: An enemy is attempting to injure you. Seeing a murder committed: Sorrow because of the actions of others.

MUSEUM:

Of a museum: Discovery of lost valuables. Visiting a museum alone: Postponement of success. Visiting a museum with a loved one: Worry will be smoothed away. Visiting a museum with family: Will realize high ambitions.

MUSIC:

Hearing melodious music: Big pleasures in life. Hearing pleasant music at a concert: Will receive some money. Enjoying good music at a theater: Consolation of misfortune. Hearing harsh and unpleasant music: Will be greatly disappointed. Hearing jazz music: Will become very uncomfortable. Hearing opera music and singing: Will hear very welcome news.

MUSTACHE:

Of a mustache: Will have disputes with a superior. A big mustache: Increase in own fortune. An ugly mustache: Will be publicly disgraced. Short mustaches: Small disagreements. A very small and thin mustache: Small money earnings. A woman admiring a mustache: She should guard her virtue. Having a mustache: Will be a betrayer of women.

MYSTERY:

Of a mystery: Something will happen that will puzzle you. A mystery being unexplained: Avoid rivals. Hearing of a mystery: You have loyal friends. Having mysterious friends: Will suffer because of own foolishness.

N

NAG:

Of nagging someone: Will receive pleasant news. Being nagged by others: Circumstances will improve. Being nagged by relatives: Loneliness and trouble. Being nagged by children: Advancement within own position.

NAKED:

A woman dreaming of being naked: Unhappiness. A man dreaming of being naked: Public disgrace. A beautiful naked woman: Good earnings. A plain naked woman: High ambitions. An ugly naked woman: Desires will not be granted. A young beautiful girl being naked: Arrogance. Wife being naked: Relatives are talking about you. Many naked women: People have a high opinion of you. Counting naked people: Will receive good news. Men and women together who are naked: Dignity. Naked people running: Loss of ambitions. Sleeping with a naked person: Big commotion. Sleeping with a naked woman away from home: Someone is doing you wrong. Walking around the streets naked: Disappointment through friends and relatives. Married people being naked: Plenty of wealth.

NECKLACE:

Of a beautiful necklace: Realization of desired love. Wearing a necklace around the neck: Abundant means.

Someone putting a necklace on you: Long married life. Losing a necklace: Will receive a visitor. Receiving a gift of a necklace: Will possess the one you love. Husband giving a necklace to his wife. Will have a luxurious home. Giving a necklace to sweetheart: Will make her a slave. A necklace for children: You are a virtuous person.

NEEDLE:

Of needles: Persecution in love. Having needles: Intrigue. A sewing needle: You love too deeply. A darning needle: You will fall in love. Knitting needles: You are too egotistic. Threading a needle: Family burdens. Searching for a needle: You worry without cause. Finding a needle: You have appreciative friends. Losing a needles: Disappointment in love. Needles made of steel: Long life. Pricking yourself with a needle: You are overly affectionate.

NEIGHBOUR:

Of a neighbour: Misfortune in business. Own neighbours: Misfortune in love. Meeting a neighbor: Will have unwelcome guests. Visiting with neighbours: Family quarrels. Socializing with neighbours: Will be embarrassed. Being very friendly with neighbours: Loss of money.

NEWSPAPER:

Reading a newspaper: Death is nearby. Others reading a newspaper to you: They are telling you untruths. A daily newspaper: Common gossip. A weekly newspaper: Advancement in business. A Sunday newspaper: Will have a short life. Buying a newspaper: Will receive a very great love. Selling a newspaper: Friends are deceiving you. Tearing a newspaper: Poverty. Throwing a newspaper away: Dishonour.

NEW YEAR:

Of the new year: An improvement in circumstances is at hand. Beginning a new year with friends: Be careful of an unscrupulous rival. Beginning an even-numbered year: Will have very little money. Beginning an odd-numbered year: Will inherit plenty of money. Being drunk at a New Year's Party: Love affairs with improve. Proposing on New Year's Eve: Marriage will last forever. Getting married on New Year's Eve: Marriage will not last long. A boy being born on New Year's Eve: Will become a prominent person. A girl being born on New Year's Eve: Will marry a wealthy person. Committing adultery on New Year's Eve: Imminent separation.

NIGHT:

Of the nighttime: Misfortune. Being in the dark: Will hear of engagement of a friend. Friends on a dark night: Will attend a funeral. Children on a dark night: Big family satisfaction. Enemies on a dark night: Embarrassment. Entering a dark place at night: Will win at gambling. House being in the dark at night: Fortune is ahead.

NOISE:

Hearing noises: People are gossiping about you. Hearing a loud noise: Quarrels among friends. Hearing a loud noise in the street: Defeat in your plans. Hearing children making noise: Will receive letter with good news. Visitors making a noise: Success in your affairs.

NOVEL:

Reading a novel: Will hear of the wedding of a relative. Writing a novel: Unhappiness. Printing a novel: Be careful of business affairs. Buying a novel: Refrain from speculation in the stock market.

NURSE:

Of a nurse: Will have a big fight. Being a wet nurse and feeding a child: Will receive unpleasant news. Nurses in a hospital: Joy and contentment. Nurses in a home: Financial damages. Needing the help of a nurse: Will be pregnant. A nurse with a doctor: Misery. Hiring a nurse: Good future. A woman dreaming of being a nurse: Will gain high position by sacrifice.

NUTRITION:

Receiving nutrition: Unhappiness. Giving children nutrition: Dignity and ambition. Giving nutrition to others: Small worries. Giving nutrition to animals: Fortune and riches.

NUTSHELL:

Of nutshells: Will have plenty of money. Cracking nutshells: Happy marriage. Stepping on nutshells: Will receive a large inheritance. Throwing away nutshells: Good luck and prosperity.

O

OASIS

Of an oasis: Will come out well from a present danger. Finding an oasis when wandering in a desert: You can rely on a friend. Being with others in an oasis: Misfortune in love affairs.

OATH:

Of taking an oath: A good position will be yours. Others taking an oath: Will receive bad news from a friend. Relatives taking an oath: Death of a relative. Business people taking an oath: Change of surrounding. Enemies taking an oath: Will suffer humiliation. Husband or wife taking a marriage oath: Prosperity. Husband and wife taking an oath after their marriage: Foretells divorce.

OBEDIENT:

Being obedient: Will have a good future. Being obedient to others: Will have a commonplace career. Others being obedient to you: Will command riches and exert wide influence. Children being obedient: Family happiness. Own help being obedient: Will make big gains in business. A woman being obedient: Brighter days are in store. A young woman being obedient: An admirer is seriously attracted to you.

OBITUARY:

Receiving obituary notice of a relative's death: Approaching money. Receiving obituary notice of a friend's death: Good news from faraway. Reading obituary notice of someone you know. News of a marriage. Reading obituary notice of an enemy: Danger in love affairs.

OBSTINATE:

Being obstinate: Will be degraded. Others being obstinate: Will have a quiet conscience. Children being obstinate: Unexpected fortune. Friends being obstinate: Will do bad business.

OCEAN:

Of the ocean: Prosperity. A calm ocean: Stormy wedded life. A rough ocean: Will have few difficulties. Having ocean waves lashing a boat: Business disaster. Being in a vessel on the open, smooth ocean: Fortunate business. Being in a vessel on the open rough ocean: Will have big troubles. Being in a vessel that sinks in the ocean: Termination of love affairs.

OFFER:

Receiving an offer: Expect an improvement in your position. Someone making a good offer to you: You will be cheated. Making an offer for services: You must work hard. making an offer to the church: Will meet with prominent personalities. Making an offer to a woman: Big friendships will develop. Making an offer to a man: Will have emotional sorrow. Making an offer to a public institution: Approaching money.

OLD:

Being old: You are being foolish. Becoming old: Will

achieve fame. Being very old: Will have bad relationship with a young woman. Having dealings with old people: Be prudent.

OLD MAN:

Of an old man: Will have troubles. Being an old man: Honour and distinction. Being a rich old man: Good health. An old man dreaming of courting an old woman: Good business enterprises.

OLD SWEETHEART:

Thinking of an old sweetheart: Happily wedded life. Embracing an old sweetheart: Will receive an unexpected gift. Making up with an old sweetheart: Will have a prominent position. Morning an old sweetheart: Family quarrels.

OPERATION:

Going to having an operation: Will have much pain. Undergoing an operation: Success will come to you. Having an operation: Beware of untrue friends. Watching an operation: Will be very lucky. Operation not being a success: Corruption. Operation being a success: You have plenty of friends. Performing an operation: Yourself wealth. Another doctor helping with an operation: You will be deceived. A nurse assisting with an operation: Success in life.

OPIUM:

Of opium: You are negligent in your affairs. Prescribing opium as medicine: Will suffer humiliation. Taking opium: Social disgrace. Taking opium with others: Bad changes in life will soon occur. Encouraging friends to take opium: Worries are ahead for you.

ORANGE:

Eating oranges: You will injure yourself. Selling oranges: True love. Buying oranges: Disappointment in love. Making orange marmalade: Death of soldiers. Of an orange tree: Will shed tears. Planting an orange tree: Will make an unsuccessful trip. Peeling oranges: Death of a relative. The color of orange: Fortune is near at hand. Orange-colored materials: Good times are coming. Buying orange-colored clothes: Small financial gains.

ORDERS:

Giving orders: Will be grateful for a service rendered to you. Obeying orders: Will have a large family. Taking orders: Sadness. Wearing military orders or medals: Will have setbacks in hopes. Giving orders to children: Advancement in love affairs. Putting things in order: Will be obedient to superiors. Ordering things through the mail: You are too gullible.

ORNAMENT:

Of ornaments: Frivolity. Wearing ornaments: High honours. Giving ornaments to others: Extravagance. Others wearing ornaments: Coming trouble. Church ornaments: Will have good spirit. Flower ornaments: Will have pleasure and fortune. Having various other kinds of ornaments: Family happiness.

OVERTAKE:

Overtaking someone else: Personal happiness. Being overtaken by others: You like to eat too much. Being overtaken by enemies: Advancement in position and good influence. Overtaking other things: Must moderate your desires.

OWL:

Of an owl: Unhappiness. Catching an owl: Happiness. Killing an owl: Great happiness. Hearing the hoot of an owl: Warning of the approach of a deceitful person. Hearing owls screaming: Someone will die.

P

PACK:

Packing for a journey: Business worries will keep you at home. Relatives packing for a trip: Happiness in the family. A woman packing clothes for a trip: She may leave her husband. A man packing clothes for a trip: He is guilty of foolish actions. Packing something to mail: Abuse of confidence.

PAIN:

Having pain in the heart: Sickness. Having pain in the teeth: Unhappiness. Having pain in the ears: Malicious gossip against you. Having pain in the stomach: Pleasant social activities. Having pain in the shoulders: Having pain in the chest: Financial gains. Having pains in the throat: Discovery of lost valuables. Having delivery pains: Death. Having pains in the legs: Will receive good news. Having pains in the feet: Will get out of trouble. Having pains all over the body: Success. Lovers dreaming of having pains all over: Their love is secured. Others being in pain: Your life is full of mistakes. Children being in pain: Persecution by an enemy.

PAPRIKA:

Of paprika: Will become very irritated. Buying paprika: Profit. Using paprika on food: Will have many pleasures in life.

PARACHUTE:

Of a parachute floating downward: Be careful not to go to extremes. Coming down in a parachute yourself: Sorrow within the family. Many people coming down in parachutes: Increase in the family. People being killed upon landing in a parachute: Dishonor for enemies.

PARENTS:

Of own parents: Will have dealings with the law. Visiting own parents: Will receive bad news. Accompanying parents: Difficult times ahead. Of parents after they are dead: Prosperity. Parents of other people: Death of a friend. A parent being naked: Big family disagreement. Being a grouchy parent: Will receive bad news. Embracing a parent: Treachery.

PARROT:

Of a parrot: Riches. Enjoying the chatter of a parrot: Flattery from a deceitful person. Children talking to a parrot: You have confidence of friends. A parrot chattering too much: Will be flattered by someone. A parrot that talks very little: Difficult work ahead. A parrot laying an egg: Increase in the family. A young engaged girl dreaming of a parrot: Inquire about fiance's family.

PARTING:

Parting with a friend: Will have a life of vexation. Parting with enemies: Success in every undertaking. Parting with relatives: Bad financial business. Parting with wife: Riches. Parting with husband: Dangers. Parting with children: Death in the family.

PARTNER:

Finding a partner: Have no fears. Having a partner: You are prone to arguing. Losing a partner: Your success is sure. Having a prominent partner: Good business.

PARTY:

Being at a party: Joy without profit. Being with others at a party: Unexpected fortune. Giving a party: Quarrels. Others giving a party for you: Disappointment in love. Being at a party without a partner: Life holds good things for you. Taking children to a party: Hopes are vanishing. Being at a wild party: Will be a victim of gossip. Someone getting hurt at a party: Will have a long life.

PEACOCK:

Of a peacock: Will be disappointed. Catching a peacock: You are too ambitious. A dead peacock: Own good plans will fail. Hearing the chirping of a peacock: A big rain will come and cause damage. The beautiful feathers of a peacock: Joy without profit. A farmer dreaming of a peacock: Will have a good harvest. A woman dreaming of a peacock circling: Riches. A man dreaming of a peacock circling: Will have troubles. A beautiful woman dreaming of a peacock: Elevation to a high position.

PEN:

Of a pen: Big unhappiness. Writing with a pen: Will receive news from absent friends. Buying a pen: Will live a long life. Writing with an old-fashioned pen: Honour. Writing with a fountain pen: You have false friends. Writing with a quill pen: People are gossiping about you. Writing love letters with a fountain pen: You are being deceived. Writing letters in bed with a pen: Annoyance. Children using a pen: Fortune in family affairs.

PERFUME:

Smelling perfume: Happiness. Spilling perfume: Loss of something that brings pleasure. Buying perfume: Will find a new lover.

PHOTOGRAPH:

Of own photograph: Misfortune in love affairs. Photographs of others: Dignity and distinction. Others taking your photograph: Will suffer loss in speculations. Taking photographs of others: A rival with take sweetheart's affection. Taking photographs of children: Approaching money. Taking photograph of relatives: Joy without profit: Taking friend's photograph: You are deceived by friends. Taking a photograph of a dead person: Happiness is assured. Having a photograph of someone dear hanging around neck: Prosperity. Receiving or giving own photograph: Treason.

PICNIC:

Of a picnic: Danger through a secret. A happy picnic: False friends are gossiping about you. Others having a picnic: Failure of enemies. Attending a picnic: Deep enjoyment of life and success. Having a picnic with children: Luck and prosperity. Having a picnic with relatives: Will realize high ambitions. Having a picnic with friends: Doubtful results in love affairs.

PEGEON:

Of pigeons: Big success. White pigeons: Consolation. Gray pigeons: Devotion. Brown and white pigeons: Good business enterprises. Many pigeons: You are engaged in charitable work. A pigeon's roost: Imminent marriage.

Pegeons flying: Good news will soon be received. Pigeons walking on the ground: Important news from faraway. Pigeons lighting on ledges: Favourable love affairs. Two pigeons fighting: Changes in own affairs.

PIMPLE:

Of pimples: Riches. Having pimples on the body: Will have good earnings. Squeezing pimples: Will have a large amount of silver.

PINK:

Of the color pink: Glorious success. Pink material of any kind: Will have a happy family life. Buying pink clothes: Recovery of lost money.

PITCHER:

Of a pitcher: Many joys and good luck. A colored pitcher: Unlucky events to come. A pottery pitcher: Will lose money. A pitcher being full: Fidelity. A pitcher being empty: Infidelity. Breaking a pitcher: Love affairs will come to an end. Throwing a pitcher away: Will have a new lover.

PITY:

Being pitied: Humiliation. Having pity for someone else: Small vexation. Having pity on relatives: Expect disappointment. Being pitied by friends: Will receive a gift. Having pity on friends: Health and joy. Having pity on poor people: Affairs are in confusion. Having pity on sick people: Luck and prosperity.

PLATFORM:

Of a platform: Will marry one you least expected. Being on a platform: Beware of hasty judgments. Performing on a platform: Death of an enemy. Making a political speech on a platform: Approaching money. Watching a parade from a platform: Triumph in love affairs.

POCKETBOOK:

Of a pocketbook: Will have emotional sorrow. Own pocketbook: Big joy. Losing a pocketbook: Quarrels with closest friends. Finding a pocketbook: Luck and prosperity. Relative's pocketbook: Discovery of a secret. A lady's pocketbook: Attainment of almost every desire.

POETRY:

Of poetry: Tranquility. Reading poetry: Happiness in love affairs. Reading poetry out loud: Death of a relative. Writing poetry: Changes in love affairs. Being a poet: Will have a hard life ahead.

POMEGRANATE:

Of a pomegranate: Will fall heir to riches. A pomegranate tree: Will receive good news. A blosoming pomegranate tree: Prosperity. A pomegranate tree with fruit on it: Joy and pleasure. Breaking a pomgranate into two pieces: Persecution from tax collector. Eating pomegranate: Hard work ahead of you. Having a basket full of pomegranates: Will be guilty of foolish actions. Pomegranates being spoiled: Troubles ahead of you.

POND:

Of a pond: Will quarrel with a loved one. A clear pond: Wealth and lasting friendship. A muddy pond: Quarrels within the home. A quiet pond: Great affection between sweethearts. A pond full of dead fish: Will soon go into bankruptcy. A pond full of live fish: Abundance and riches. A dry pond:

Poverty. A very small pond: You are surrounded by much gossip. A very big pond: Good times are coming.

PONY:

Of a pony: Will marry a beautiful girl. A beautiful pony: Will acquire a beautiful house. An ugly pony: Will marry an ugly wife. A newly born pony: Will have a woman who loves you very much. Pony running: Hard work ahead. Several ponies: Investments will bring profits. Buying a pony: Embarrassment. Selling a pony: Unpleasant news. Feeding a pony in your hand: Will be kissed by a woman. Children playing with a pony: Will be seduced by a woman. Children riding ponies: Will be freed of bad accusations.

POOL:

Of a pool: Fortune is ahead of you. A pool of water: Will have good business. A pool with very little water: Refrain from stock market speculation. A dirty pool: Prosperous business. A dry pool: Will forgive your enemies.

POST OFFICE:

Of a post office: Will be offended by someone. Being in a post office: Will be victorious through honesty. Mailing a letter at the post office: Will have obstacles in your path. Receiving a letter from the post office: Change of residence. Registering a letter from the post office. Change of companions. Buying stamps at a post office: Unpleasant things awaiting. Finding post office closed: Dissension in love affairs.

POVERTY:

Being in poverty: Will soon incur a loss. Other people in poverty: Will give beneficial service to others. Many people in poverty: Unpleasant family affairs. Crippled people in poverty: Love argument. Falling into poverty: Will have many children. Being in poverty and very sick: Will have many debts to pay. Family falling into poverty: Future riches. Friends being in poverty: Health and joy.

PRAISE:

Receiving praise: Are surrounded by scandal. Giving praise: People are gossiping about you. Hearing others praise you: You have faithful friends. Praising God: Abundant means. Praising your children: Jealousy by other members of family.

POWER:

Being powerful: Will have a big loss. Having power in your position: Good future. Taking advantage of your power: Will receive good news. Using your powers to hurt others: Will fall into disgrace. Own power going to your head: You will go crazy.

PRAY:

Of praying: Honours and riches. Praying in church: Desires will be accomplished. Praying to God: Much happiness. Praying to Jesus Christ: Riches. Praying to the cross of Jesus Christ: Infidelity. Praying for someone else: Poverty. Other people praying for you: Happiness. Praying for someone who has died: Will affair your desires. Praying and having prayer heard: Fortune. Praying and it not being heard: Misfortune. Praying to possess a lady: Good reputation. Praying for someone to do something for you: Bad consequences.

PREGNANT:

Being pregnant: Health will soon improve. A married woman dreaming of being pregnant: Marital unhappiness. Unmarried woman dreaming of being pregnant: Trouble and injury through scandal. A man dreaming that his wife is pregnant: She will give a birth to a boy. A widow dreaming of being pregnant: She will marry very soon. A widower dreaming of a pregnant woman: Will have plenty of money. A young girl dreaming of being pregnant: Won't get married for long time. A young man dreaming of getting a girl friend pregnant: Remorse of conscience.

PRESENT:

Receiving a present: Will have pleasant reunion with a friend. Receiving a present from a loved one: Success and good luck. Receiving a present from others: Bad luck. Receiving several presents: Beware of person from whom you received them. Giving a present to a relative: Good hopes. Receiving a present from an important person: Will receive many honours. Receiving a present from relatives: Postponement of success. Receiving a Christmas gift from relatives: Will have many admirers. Receiving a Christmas present from friends: Tearson.

PRINCE:

Of a prince: A present will be given to you. Meeting a prince: Honours and riches to come. Going with a prince: Will have a large fortune. Asking permission for audience with a prince: Success in business. Killing a prince: Will receive news of the death of a loved one. Talking with a princess: Will have self-conceit. Seeing a princess: Will be very arrogant with friends. Residing with a princess: Peril of death.

PRINTER:

Of a printer: Hidden family secrets. Being a printer: Must exercise extreme economy. Others who are printers: Will experience poverty. A relative who is a printer: Family fortune. Printers in the printing business: Decline in business.

PRIZE:

Receiving a prize: You fear an enemy. Giving a prize: Good friendship. Others receiving a prize: Infirmity. Friends receiving a prize: Will have an illness in the family. Enemy receiving a prize: Beware of gossip.

PROSPERITY:

Of prosperity: Marriage to a wealthy person. Looking at property: Riches. Receiving property as a gift: Will have agreeable conditions. Giving a gift of property: Will have a big family. Buying property: Will have plenty of wealth. Selling property: Will marry a young person. A prospective buyer of property: You are a dreamer. Having a business on own property: Will receive wonderful news. Selling property in the country: Disgrace. Possessing property in the country: Fortune. Having a large estate of property: Unhappiness. Inheriting property: Will be in mourning.

PROUD:

Of being pround: Doomed for disappointment. Being pround of family: A false friend is nearby. Being pound of work: You are prone to being a know-it-all. Being proud of having a good business: Failure of enemies.

PURPLE:

Of the color purple: Will take a joyful journey. Having a purple dress: Happy marriage. Having a purple coat and hat:

Honour. Having purple flowers: Loss of own estate. Having purple materials: Loss of friends.

PURSE:

Of a purse: Happiness. Finding a purse without money: Mis-understanding between relatives. Finding a purse with money in it: Increase in the family. Lovers dreaming of finding a purse: Happy life. Lovers dreaming of losing a purse: Expect difficulties or illness. Buying a purse: Will attend a wedding. Receiving a purse as a gift: Carelessness. Giving a purse as a gift: Will accomplish your goals.

Q

QUARREL:

Starting a quarrel: Prosperity in business affairs. Quarreling with wife or husband: Will be quilty of foolish actions. Quarreling with a sweetheart: Will make up very soon. Quarreling with a friend: Loss of money. Having a family quarrel: Opposition to face at home. Having a quarrel with a partner: Will have mastery over many matters. Having business quarrels: Warning of trouble.

QUEEN:

Of a queen: Deceit in love affairs. Sending a letter to a queen: Danger. Going to see a queen: Good fortune. Having an interview with a queen: Rebellion within the home. A queen surrounded by her court: Will be deceived by friends. A madonna queen of the church: Will be pardoned of your sins.

QUEUE:

Of a queue: Re-established friendship. Waiting in a queue: Will lead to marriage. Being in a queue with your family. Be on guard against spiteful gossip. Others in a queue: Important event very beneficial.

R

RABBIT:

Of a rabbit: Failure of enemies. A rabbit running: Change of occupation. Several rabbits on the sun: Very good business ventures. Eating rabbit: Will quarrel with a friend. Shooting rabbits: Happiness. Having rabbits in own back yard: Great friendship.

RAIN:

Of rain: Abundant means. Hearing patter of rain on the roof: Great marital happiness. Getting wet in a downpour of rain: Suffering caused by suspicion of friends. Rain dripping into a room: Beware of false friends. A farmer dreaming of rain without with or storm: Good earnings and profits. A businessman dreaming of rain: Misfortune in business. A big downpour of rain and bad wind: Look out for rivals. A very bad rain-and windstorm: Great joy. Rich people dreaming of a downpour with hail: Affiction in love. Poor people dreaming of rain with hail: Good opportunities and happy life. Women being out in the rain: Disappointment in love. Others being out in the rain: Great sorrow. A rain-and hailstorm ruining crops: Abundant means ahead.

RAPE:

Of rare items: You have a highly egotistic nature. Rare gems: Will have affiction and uneasiness. Buying rare items:

Will have big disputes with friends. Eating rare meat: Joy and prosperity. Eating rare vegetables: Will argue with the one you love. Children eating rare food: Will collect money.

RECEIVE:

Receiving a love letter: Unhappiness and persecution. Receiving a gift at own house: Will have good hopes. Receiving a ring as a gift secretly: Will have a promise of matrimony. Receiving important personalities at own house: Riches. Being received by other people: You lead a very carefree life.

RELATIVE:

Of relatives: Will receive bad news. Discussing matters with relatives: Bad luck to come. Embracing a relative: Treachery. Relatives being naked: Will have a very bad quarrel. Talking with relatives: Big disappointment in family affairs. Receiving invitation from relative: Beware of why they are inviting you. Entertaining relatives: Danger is ahead. Eating with relatives: Death in the family.

RESTAURANT:

Of a restaurant: Bad health. Entering a restaurant: Friendship. Eating at a restaurant: Health is not very good. Eating with children at a restaurant: Wealth. Others eating at a restaurant: Will receive money soon. Eating with relatives in a restaurant: Will overcome enemies with patience. Eating at a restaurant with sweetheart: Bad financial condition. Enemies eating in a restaurant: Will become rich by economy. Husband and wife eating in a restaurant alone: Long happy marriage.

RETURN:

Of returning: Unexpected joy. Returning from a trip:

Great prosperity. Others returning after a long time: Losses soon to be made good. Relatives returning from a trip: Jealousy within the family. Friends returning to their home: Treachery. Sweetheart returning home: He has been untrue to you.

REVOLVER:

Handling a revolver: Danger from water. Using a revolver: Profit. Firing a revolver: You will be cheated. Children holding a revolver: Parents are unworthy. Killing with a revolver: Will have a long life. Enemies using a revolver: Return of good health. Officers with a revolver: Good harvest. Policemen using a revolver: Will receive good news from abroad.

RICH:

Being rich: High honours and success. Becoming rich: Will receive a big reward. Not becoming rich: Will obtain small employment under wealthy person. Others who are rich: Turmoil in business affairs. Other people becoming rich: Affairs are flourishing. Talking with rich people: Will have beneficial compensation. Relatives being rich: They will have trouble in their life. Children becoming rich: Change in environment.

RING:

Of several rings: Large quarrel. Wearing a ring: Troubles caused by a friend. Receiving a ring as a gift: Matrimony in the near future. Having a diamond ring: Great riches. Having a ring of precious stones: Wealth. An unmarried person dreaming of a ring with precious stones: Matrimony. Married person dreaming of ring of precious stones: Birth of a child. Having a large ring covered with diamonds: Will receive high honours. Having a gold ring: Dignity. Having a gold ring put on your finger: Honour and riches. Having an iron ring: Hard work ahead. Losing your ring: Big fortune. A single girl dreaming of losing her ring: She'll be left by boyfriend. A man dreaming of losing his ring: Fieance will marry another man. Receiving several rings: Security in love. Buying a ring: Will be an important person. Giving a gift of rings: Loss of money. Ring being broken: Domestic unrest. Fieancee ring being broken: Separation of lovers. Receiving a wedding ring: Will have a devoted lover. Breaking a wedding ring: Divorce. Having a ring on a chain: Good health. Making a ring from your own hair: Declaration of love. Giving or receiving a ring made from hair: Marriage.

RIOT:

Of a riot: Financial failure. Taking part in a riot: Misfortune in business. Friends taking part in a riot: Persecution by an enemy. Enemies taking part in a riot: Will receive money. Relatives taking part in a riot: Death of a friend. A riot ending: Will receive high honours.

ROCKET:

Of a rocket: Short-lived success. Building a rocket: Must have firmer foundations for business. Throwing a rocket: Abundant means. Enemies being killed by a rocket: Will hear false news. Exploding a rocket: Fortune in the family. Many rockets: Triumph over enemies.

ROSE:

Of roses: Happiness. Holding roses in hands during season: Joy. Smelling roses during season: Happy news. Sick people holding or smelling roses in season: Danger of death. Holding roses out of season: Misfortune. Picking roses: Will have a proposal of marriage. Rose blossoms being withered and falling away: You are deceived. Slightly faded roses: Success will come after some difficulties. White roses: Innocence. Red roses: Will be a bachelor or lod maid. Giving roses as a gift: Modestry. Receiving roses as a gift: Pleasant memories of old friends. Picking roses: You are a good lover or sweetheart. Deep-red roses: Joyous times and fun. Rose buds: Riches. Picking rose buds: Increase in the family.

RUBBER:

Of rubber: Prosperity. Using rubber for various things: Will take a long trip. Articles made from rubber: Rebellion among relatives. Erasing writing with a rubber: Uncertainly in actions. Erasing love letters with a rubber: You are giving a lover the brushoff.

RUBY:

Of rubies: Happiness. Wearing jewelry with rubies: Will triumph over enemies. Wearing a ruby ring: Will have a very faithful love. Buying jewelry with rubies in it: Consolation. Selling ruby jewelry: Loss of money.

S

SACRIFICE:

Making a sacrifice: Changes in environment. Others making a sacrifice for you: Big joy. Friends making a sacrifice for you: Approaching money. Relatives making a sacrifice for you: Recovery of money.

SAD:

Being sad yourself: Lasting joy. Children being sad: Good fortune in the future. Wife or husband being sad: Good times are coming. Relatives being sad: Family quarrels.

SAILING:

Of sailing a boat: Happiness. A sailor sailing boat: Financial gains. Sweetheart sailing alone: Will have emotional sorrow. Sailing a very small boat yourself: Big success in everything. A sailboat sailing in a calm sea: Death of a friend. Sailing a boat in a stormy sea: Lasting joy. Children sailing a small boat: Will have mastery over many matters.

SALARY:

Receiving a salary: Big joy ahead for you. Paying salary: Hard work awaits you. Others collecting their salary: Triumph over enemies. Others paying salary: Beware of jealous friends. Paying a salary to your help: Financial gains.

SANDAL:

Of sandals: Will have good health. Wearing sandals: Will have healthy feet. Taking off sandals: Will receive small unexpected inheritance from stranger. Changing sandals: Will have a headache. Throwing away sandals: Will receive an unexpected gift.

SAPPHIRE:

Of sapphires: Will be happy. A woman dreaming of wearing sapphire rings: She will be molested. A woman dreaming of dark blue sapphires: Husband will bring great happiness. Other people wearing sapphire rings: Disputes with best friends. Wearing jewelry with sapphire stones: Will be seduced by force. Wearing sapphire bracelets: You have many secret enemies. Friends wearing sapphire rings: Will receive very pleasant news.

SAVINGS:

Of financial savings: Will have good friendships. Putting money in a savings account: You eat good foods. Having plenty of money in a savings account: Will surprise your enemies. Others accumulating savings: Poverty. Children saving money: Family secret will be revealed.

SCANDAL:

Of a scandal: Honour and triumph. Being involved in a scandal: Will be offended. Hearing of scandals: Will receive a marriage proposal. Friends being involved in a scandal: Financial gains. Enemies being involved in a scandal: Prosperity. Farmers being involved in a scandal: Will have a good harvest.

SCENT:

Smelling a bad scent: Loss of friendship with neighbours. Smelling a bad scent in the air: Will be deceived by best friend. Smelling scent of bad breath: Someone will trick you. Smelling a perfume scent: Prostitution. Having a bottle of perfume: Corruption. Smelling perfume on others: Loss of friendship. Smelling perfume on friends: Revelation of a secret. Buying perfume: Will have a good harvest. Going into a store selling perfume: Unexpected business transaction.

SCHOOL:

Of a school: Will suffer humiliation. Going to school: Business will be in good standing. Taking children to school: Will set a good example for children. Children going to school alone: Family disagreement. Children getting good grades at school: Family happiness. Going to high school: Modestry. Spending money for schooling: You are surrounded by boisterous people. Being in school yourself: Increase of knowledge. Children becoming teachers: You have promising business affairs. Going to elementary school: Will do crazy things. Going to grammar school: Anxiety. Going to a swimming school: Will soon be robbed. Going to a dancing school: Your morals make you unfit to fill position.

SELL:

Of selling: Will make money. Selling things of steel: Will fall into disgrace. Selling small quantities of merchandise: Abundance and riches. Selling milk and cheese: Unexpected big fortune. Selling tobacco: Will have many worries. Selling mechanical things: Unhappiness. Selling property: Illness. Selling jewelry: Will be loved. Selling a business: Will have family arguments.

SEPARATION:

Of a separation : Frivolity. Husband and wife separating: Gossip by friends. Separation of sweethearts: Idle talk by people around you. Planning on separating from someone: Misfortune awaits. Having a final separation: Will be guilty of foolish actions. Others desiring your separation: Beware of shady people. Separation of children's marriage: Inheritance. Friends being separated: Sickness of children. Sweetheart wanting a separation: Be cautious in business transactions. Separating from a business partner: Success in business. Separating from those you love: Failure of some cherished plan.

SHAWL:

Of a shawl: Someone will be cruel to you. Wearing a shawl: Will have success in love. Buying a shawl: Will receive a visit from a doctor. Wearing embroidered shawl given as a gift: Unjustified gossip about you. Relatives wearing a shawl: Will go to a funeral parlor. Friends wearing a shawl: Must pay more attention to business. Poor people wearing shawls: Enemies are plotting against you. Young girls wearing shawls: You are surrounded by fast-talking people. A large white shawl: Purity and virtue. A black shawl: Grief. A red shawl: You are too loose with your affections. Various other colored shawls: Affairs will run smoothly. Giving a shawl as a gift: Will have deep affection from one you love.

SHIP:

Of a ship: Prosperity. A prisoner dreaming of a ship: Will be released. A man dreaming of a ship docking: Unexpected good news. A woman dreaming of a ship docking: Unexpected bad news. Lovers dreaming of a ship docking: Marriage will not be realized. A ship sinking:

Abundance of money. A ship sinking after a collision: Good ventures in the future. Two ships going in opposite directions: Promotion and honour.

SHOCK:

Of a shock: Will overcome enemies with perseverance. Being shocked by bad news: Will have mastery over own affairs. Shocking members of own family: Will overcome difficulties. Being shocked by a loved person: Good luck. Shocking a loved one: Your love is very changeable. Shocking other people: Beware of a trap being laid for you.

SHORT:

Of being short of everything: Will have happiness in old age. Being short of money: Postponement of success. Being short of food: Good improvements financially. Being short in weight: An enemy is seeking your ruin. Being short of belongings: Good days are coming. Being short in conversation: Progress in business enterprises. Having short clothes or trousers: Warning of trouble.

SHOWER:

Taking a shower: Abundance. Children taking a shower: Will receive a gift. Guests going to take a shower: Loss of money. Others taking a shower: Riches.

SHY:

Being shy: Furtune ahead. Make being shy: You trust relatives too much. Children being shy: You are surrounded by jealous people. Others being shy: Plans will turn out unsatisfactory.

SICK:

Being sick: You are inclined to being melancholy. Children being sick: Happiness. Visiting sick people: Will find a way to reach your goal. Loved ones who are sick: Unhappiness. Many sick people: Joy and profit. Being mentally sick: Fortune will be lost. Being sick to the stomach: Squandering of possessions. Visiting sick people at a hospital: Life will offer many pleasures.

SIGN:

Of signing: Big success. Signing a legal document: Will abandon the family home. Signing a contract: Someone will confide a secret to you. Other people signing papers: Will have a good position. Signing an agreement: You are an idealist. Signing a letter: Will make new friends. Signing an unpleasant: Will attain aim in life. Signing a check: Avoid squandering money. Signing a love letter: Beware of untruthful people. Signing a note to borrow money: Will make new acquaintances. Making signs with hands: Beware of being seduced. Making signs with fingers: Vanity.

SKELETON:

Of a skeleton: Will have spells of nausea. Being a skeleton: Domestic troubles. A skeleton of ancestors: Death in the family. A skeleton of an animal: Will have fear because of wrongdoing. A skeleton of someone you know: Danger or illness.

SLIPPERS:

Of slippers: Contentment in own heart. Wearing slippers: Security. An unmarried person dreaming of wearing slippers: Be careful in choice of mate. Slippers for woman: Will have to pardon enemies. A woman wearing slippers: Good financial position. Buying slippers: Will receive a small kindness. Having many slippers: Will receive a large reward.

SMART:

Being smart: You have many good friends. Having a smart mate: Happy events to come. Having smart children: Small family arguments. Having smart friends: Triumph and honour.

SMILE:

Of smiling: Will be relieved of pains. Family smiling: Will suffer opposition for forty-eight to seventy days. Friends smiling: Beware: they may not be true friends. Children smiling: Riches. Husband smiling: He has made good money. Wife smiling at her husband: Will tell him of pregnancy.

SNAKE:

Of snakes: Your plans will be wrecked. A coilled snake: Will escape from danger. A snake ready to strike: Treachery from one you least expect. Killing a snake: Will have victory over enemies. Several snakes: Jeslous people would like to cause your ruin. Being unable to kill a snake: Unfortunate events that were not anticipated. A snake with two heads: Seduction. A water snake: Will recover from an illness. Snakes being in a cage at a zoo: Your friends are not grateful.

SNEEZE:

Of sneezing: Will live a long life. Sneezing many times: Will fall in love. Babies sneczing: Will have minor stomach trouble. Children sneezing: Beware of injury to children. Others sneezing: Disaster.

SOPE:

Of soap: Bad business. Buying soap: Business affairs are all confused. Selling soap: Loss of business. Washing own body with soap: Will ask for help from friends.

SOLD:

Having sold something: You have been cheated. Having sold own belongings: Unhappiness and uneasiness. Having sold something too cheap: Will have many regrets. A poor man having sold to a rich man too cheaply: Will have more money.

SON:

Having one son: Will soon become pregnant. Having several sons: Success in business. Giving birth to a son when not pregnant: Happiness. Adopting a son: Onw children will dislike the adopted son. A son being killed: Misery caused by parents. Talking to own son: Losses in business. Rescuing your son from danger: He will rise to eminence. Own son being sick: Obstacles are ahead for you. Own son being crippled: Trouble awaits.

SORROW:

Of sorrow: Will receive sad news. Having sorrow because of loss: Good times are coming. Being sorrowful over the loss of a relative: Approaching money. Being sorrowful over the loss of a loved one: Change for the better. Being sorrowful over the loss of a sweetheart: Immediate success. Being sorrowful over the loss of husband: Be careful with investments. Being sorrowful over the loss of life: Financial gains.

SPARROW:

Of a sparrow: Hard work is ahead for you. Many sparrows: Death of an enemy. Catching a sparrow: Big success in business. Feeding sparrows: Danger in love affairs. Killing a sparrow: Secret enmity of some person for you.

SPEAK:

Of speaking: You enjoy many kinds of entertainment. Speaking with own mother: Will have good news. Husband and wife speaking to each other: Beware of gossip by neighbours. A man dreaming of speaking to a woman: Good ventures in business affairs. A woman dreaming of speaking to a man: Submit yourself to the man's will. Speaking to a friend: Suffering to come. Speaking to an enemy: Family quarrels. Speaking to a dog or parrot: Death.

SPECTACLES:

Of spectacles: Will live to a ripe old age. Wearing spectacles: Will come out well from a present peril. Buying spectacles: Financial conditions will rise. Broken spectacles: Beware of passions leading you astray. Enjoying a theatrical spectacle: Beware of double dealings by strangers. An appealing dramatic spectacle: Small changes in your life. Seeing a good play with a loved one: Matrimony.

SPEND:

Spending money: Enjoyable entertainment. Spending money in traveling: Frivolity. Spending money on the family: Loss of good friends. Spending money for food: Will have happy days. Spending money on children: Will give service to an ungrateful person. Spending money to travel: Short-lived love affair. Spending money for amousements: Will quarrel will friends. A man spending money on his wife: Family consolation. A man spending money on other women: Will desert his home A woman spending money on a man: Will have a guilty conscience. A woman spending money on her family: Blessings from God. Spending money foolishly: Be careful and economize for a short time. Spending money for charity: Affairs will improve after a long while.

SPINNING:

Of spinning cotton: Wealth. Spinning wool: Don't neglect children if they are to become prominent. A spinner at work: Will have good earnings. Operating a spinning wheel: Will not be recompensed for own diligence. Owning a spinning wheel: New acquaintances may prove untrustworthy. An old woman dreaming of spinning: Annoyance and anxiety.

SPY:

Of a spy: You desired to render a service, but offer was refused. Being a spy: Adventures will come your way. Recognizing a spy: Protect yourself from bad influences. Dealing with a spy: Business will run smoothly.

STAGE:

Of a stage: Remarkable events to come. The floor of a stage: You love pleasures too much. Being on a stage: Disappointment in projects begun. Building a stage: Will mourn over the loss of relatives. Sitting in a box near the stage: Will endure terrible pains. Being thrown out of a stage door: Will have pains in the heart.

STAIRS:

Of a broad staircase: Wealth and honour. Very high stairs: Will be jilted by your lover. Becoming dizzy on the stairs: Important and very beneficial event to come. Falling from the stairs: Own envy will cause suffering. Climbing stairs: Unusual happiness and prosperity. Climbing stairs with others: You have loyal friends. Descending stairs: Disappointments in business. Descending stairs with others: Danger through a secret.

STARVE:

Of starving: Will acquire riches through courage. Eating while dreaming of starving: Will become very rich. Suffering from starvation: Much wealth is coming to you. Starving for several days: Success in business and wordly affairs. Others starving: Abundant means.

STATUE:

Of statues: Unhappiness. Adoring a statue: Big sorrow. A statue moving: Riches. A statue of a saint: Wealth. A statue of a naked woman: Honour and distinction. A statue of a naked man: Good results in own enterprises. Several statues: Your love is not wanted.

STERILE:

Being sterile: Will receive sad news. Mates discussing inability to have children: Will adopt a child. Members of family being sterile: Domestic happiness. Friends who are sterile: You are too generous with loved ones.

STICK:

Having a stick in your hand: Unhappiness. Leaning on a stick: Sickness. Hitting someone with a strong stick: Will be dominated by a woman. Hitting strangers with a stick: Profit and good news. Hitting relatives with a stick: Good hopes. Pressing gunpowder into a gun with a stick: Will enjoy better days.

STOCK MARKET:

Of a stock market: Poverty. Being at the stock market: Death of a friend. Dealing in stocks: Patience will be advantageous. Making gains at the stock market: Will enjoy peace of mind. Losing at the stock market: Abundance and riches. Being a member of the stock market: Will have dealings with debtors.

STORE:

Of a store: Increased wealth. Having a store: Don't squander your money. Being in a store: Avoid rivals. Buying things in a department store: Joy without profit. Buying food at a grocery store: A mystery will be solved.

STORM:

Of a storm: Unfortunate business undertakings will cause distress. Watching a storm: Unhappiness in love. Being in a storm: Separation of loved ones. Others being in a storm: Change for the better. A storm hitting own house: Discovery of a secret. A storm demolishing your house: People with evil intentions are nearly. A storm damaging your house: Will have good morals. A storm demolishing the homes of others: Big dangers ahead.

STORY:

Hearing a story: Will have much hard work ahead. Reading a story: Wishes will be realized. Writing a story: Unhappiness and weakness of mind. Others writing a story: Arguments within the family. Selling a story to a magazine: Beware of being seduced.

STRANGLE:

Of strangling: Troubles. Being strangled: A false friend

is nearby. Strangling someone yourself: Your wish will come true. Others being strangled: Rapid success of own hopes.

STRAW:

Of straw: Difficulties and poverty. Having straw: Joy. Cutting straw: Will have much pain. Straw in a bundle: Security in your business. Several bundles of straw: Joy and honour. Straw in a stable: Happiness in domestic matters. Burning straw: Will attend a big festivity. Selling straw: Prosperity.

STRING:

Of String: You have a strong power of attraction. Having string: Will have quarrels and danger.

STRIP:

Being stripped: You have a great desire to do good for others. Stripping yourself: Will have quarrels. Others who are stripped: Arrival of a friend. A woman of ill fame stripping herself: Unhappiness. Being stripped by force: Will receive good advice.

STRUCTURE:

Of a big structure: Good furtune in married life. A small structure: Beware of relatives. A structure being built: Will be badly treated by creditors. Being inside a structure: Your future is secured. Being outside a structure: Will work hard all during life.

STUDY:

Of studying: Will have a clear consciene. Children studying: All desires will be realized. Children not studying: Will abuse the confidence of others. A mate studying: Will have an unhappy married life: A professor studying: Will receive a proposal of marriage.

SUICIDE:

Of a suicide: You have overstrained your mind. Planning to commit suicide: Troubles were brought on by yourself. Having committed suicide: Unhappiness. Thinking of committing suicide: Must confirm yourself to real to real life. A woman committing suicide: Opposition in love and despair. Others committing suicide: Will live a long life. A husband or life committing suicide: Permanent change in surroundings.

SUNSHINE:

Of the sunshine: Will have a long and happy life. Sunshine being very hot: Will have ups and downs in life. Sunshine being obsecured by a cloud: Will fall in love. The sunshine first thing in the morning: Will receive good news from farwawy.

SURRENDER:

Surrendering to a lover: Will become even more stingy in the future. Surrendering to the police: Will receive good news. Surrendering to the will of your mate: Will have big earnings. Surrendering stolen items: Must endure several sleepless nights. An army surrendering: Unhappiness.

SUSPEND:

Being suspend from your job: Success in new enterprises. Suspending others from their job: Will incur many debts. Being suspended in the air: Will enjoy honour and consideration by others. Others being suspended in the air: Sickness.

SWEAR:

Of swearing: Watch your actions. Having sworn: Will receive bad news. Others sweraing: Will be blamed for your actions. Relatives swearing: Will receive unpleasant news.

SWEETHEART:

Of a sweetheart: Will have a difficult experience. Having a pleasing and beautiful sweetheart: Watch rivals. Having a handsome sweetheart: Watch him very closely. Having a changeable sweetheart: Loss of love.

SWIM:

Of swimming: Will have love and pleasure. Swimming on your back: Will have a big quarrel. Swimming in the open sea: Prosperity. Swimming in a river: Will encounter danger in the near future. Swimming in muddy water: Your path is beset with many obstacles. Swimming in a pool: Success. Swimming to a shore: Hard work is ahead for you. Swimming and reaching your objective: Will be successful in everything.

T

TABLE:

Of a table : Joy. A mahoganytable: Recovery from an illness. A banquet table: Enjoyment in life. A table with a marble top: Will have a comfortable life. A broken table: Misery and poverty. Breaking a table: Loss of furtune: An empty table: Will fall into poverty. Being seated at a table: Happiness. Sitting at a table with own family: Happy married life. Friends seated at a table: Accord among friends. Children seated at a table: Luck and prosperity. Relatives seated at a table: Change in environment. Convention people seated at a table: Change for the better. Marriage quests seated at a table: Happiness is assured. Sitting at a table with sweetheart: Triumph over enemies.

TAILOR:

Of a tailor: Congenial work and good news. A male tailor: Exercise caution in business ventures. A female tailor: Avoid rivals. A girl dreaming of a tailor: She will marry a man beneath her standing. Being a tailor: Change of surroundings. Becoming a tailor: Good times are coming. Ordering clothes from a tailor: Joy without profit.

TALK:

Of talking: You are confronted with insturmountable obstacles. Talking too much: Will be exposed to some malicious plans. Hearing much talking around you: Be careful of neighbours. Husband and wife talking very loud: Family difficulties. Hearing relatives talking to you: Warning of troubles. Talking to a business partner: An enemy is seeking your ruin. Talking will friends: Will come out well from present peril. Talking to an enemy: Embarrassment. Talking to mother and father: Will be granted what you asked for. Talking to a sweetheart: Beware of jealous friends. Talking to a woman: Good success in your business. Talking to your superior: Will become a victim and suffer humiliation. Talking to a dog: Unhappiness. Talking to a parrot and other animals: Death of a friend.

TARGET:

Of a target: Will fully succeed in getting what you desired. Shooting at a target: Architectural plans need your attention. Making a bull's-eye on a target: Happiness is assured. Missing a target completely: Death of an enemy.

TEA:

Of tea: Dignity and distinction: Buying tea: Will experience many ups and downs soon. Making tea: Be cautious in your dealings because of an indiscreet act. Drinking tea: Domestic unhappiness. Drinking tea with others: Will live a long life. Drinking tea at a teashop: Financial gains. Drinking tea at a large party: You are being deceived. Tea grounds: Will have many social duties. Tea bags: Will be disappointed in a love affair.

TEACHER:

Of a teacher: Will be invited to a solemn occasion. Being a teacher: Will have sorrow. Teaching classes: Must control your passions. Teaching small children: You have a loyal friend. Teaching night school: A change in life will soon come. Being taught: Anger over a small trifling will you. Teaching only men: Danger through a secret. Teaching only women: Will be cheated by friends.

TEARS:

Of tears: Opposition will end with happiness. Crying: Will receive a gift: Children shedding tears: Recovery of money due you. Husband shedding tears: Happiness in marriage. Sweetheart shedding tears: Will have consolation. Relatives shedding tears: Will soon experience many ups and downs in affairs.

TEETH:

Of teeth: Be careful of your health. White teeth: A wish will be realized. A gold tooth: Corruption and sorrow. A tooth of any other metal: Humiliation. Infected teeth: Must give much explanation to other people. Having black teeth: Sickness of a relative. Having dirty teeth: Prosperity. Not brushing teeth: Faithful friends. Brushing teeth of children: Will borrow money from relatives.

TEMPLE:

A temple in your own country: Death of a very close friend. A temple in a foreign country: Unusual experience is coming to you. Going into a temple: Discretion will bring rewards. Idols in a temple: Will do something unjustified.

THEFT:

Of a theft: Will incur big damages. Being robbed: An early marriage. Committing a theft: Loss of money on business ventures. Stealing clothing: Loss of friends. Stealing food: Will suffer a financial lose. Stealing money: Hard days ahead.

THORN:

Of thorns: Will enjoy much contenment. Being pricked by a thorn: Warning of trouble. Children being pricked by a thorn: Change of surroundings. Being irritated by a thorn Change for the better: Having thorns on your body: Sickness.

THUNDER:

Of a thunderstorm: Will have financial troubles. Rich people dreaming of thunder: Affliction. Poor people dreaming of thunder: Imminent perils. Lightning following thunder: Death of a friend. Being hit by lighting following thunder: A woman who is overly sexual.

TIGER:

Of a tiger: Enemies will beset your path. Watching a tiger: Family fortune. A tiger running: Serious illness. Killing a tiger Beware of jealous friends. A tiger dying when delivering babies: Will receive money. A tiger performing at a circus: Will have helpful friends. Being surprised by a tiger: Will suffer great embarrassment. Having a small tiger as a pet: Will receive a marriage proposal. A tiger in a cage at the zoo: Death of a prominent person. Hearing a tiger roaring: Will suffer giref. A tiger being tied with a chain: Will be surprised by an enemy. A tiger eating: Will have much wealth.

TOOTHACHE:

Having a toothache: Will receive good news from faraway. Children having a toothache: Happiness over letter from an old friend. Having a persisting toothache: Fortune in the future. Going to a dentist to cure toothache: You have no idea what love means. Receiving relief from a toothache:

Love quarrels.

TOYS:

Of toys: Will have happy family. Giving toys to children: Good timesare coming. Buying toys: Children will be clever and successful. Receiving toys for your children: You have loyal friends. Broken toys: Approaching illness.

TRAIN:

Of a train: Will take care of business with speed. A mail train: Will enjoy very good business. A cargo train: Will meet a pleasant person. Travelling on a train alone: A lawsuit will be ruled in your favour. Travelling on a train with the family: Advantages in life. Travelling on a train with friends: Financial gains. Having a long train on a dress: Unhappiness. Someone stepping on the train of your dress: Will have a new love affair.

TRAVEL:

Of travelling: Difficulties in business ventures. Travelling alone: Will avoid unpleasant events. Travelling with your family: Will avoid unhappiness. Travelling with loved one: Delays in personal matters. Travelling with friends: Someone is cheating you. Travelling with business associates: Disappointments in all affairs. Travelling with others: Quarrels among friends. Travelling on a train: Think before you act. Travelling in a carriage: Will enjoy large fortune. Travelling in a car: HPPINESS and family LOVE. Travelling on a horse: Will have dealings with obstinate people. Travelling on foot: Hard work is ahead for you. Travelling to foreign countries: Consider results before acting. Travelling from your own town to another: Small success. Travelling from another town to your own: Success depends upon hard work. Travelling with fire-arms: Will soon find a wife. Travelling with a sword at your side: Will soon get married.

TWINS:

Having twins: HAPPINESS in the family. A woman dreaming of having twins: Avoid rivals. A man dreaming of wife having twins: Change of surroundings. Having twins of the same sex: Will live a long life. Having twins of a different sex: Dignity and distinction. An unmarried woman dreaming of having twins: Will soon be engaged. Having twin horses: Will come out well from a present peril.

U

UMBRELLA:

Having an umbrella: Will have prosperity. Carrying an umbrella: Will be annoyed by trouble and many vexations. Carrying an open umbrella over the head: Someone will come to your aid. Having an umbrella open inside the house: Big misfortune. Others with an umbrella: Birth of a child. Others with a closed umbrella: Sickness. Borrowing an umbrella: Will have misunderstandings with a friend. Lending an umbrella: Will be hurt by untrue friends. An umbrella leaking: Will be displeased with your lover.

UNDERSS:

Being undressed: Gossip and malice will cause sorrow. Undressing yourself: Will have happiness in the near future. Undressing in privacy: A guarded secret will be discovered. Undressing before others: People are talking badly behind your back. Others undressing: Will be visited by a loved one. Undressing in another's house: Will receive plenty of money. Undressing in a hotel room: Satisfaction in love. Undressing children: Pleasant events will occur in your life. Husband and wife undressing in same room: Business affairs will go bad. Undressing in public: Distress will come to you.

UNMARRIED:

Married people dreaming of being single: Dangerous jealously. Single man dreaming of remaining single: Will secure a good business, venture. A single person desiring to get married: Will receive good news. A young girl desiring to get married: She is truthful and trustworthy. An old bachelor wanting to get married: Will marry a healthy woman. An old maid wanting to get married: She will marry a young man.

URN:

Of a urn: Will receive news from a new acquaintance. Putting hands in an urn: Good business. Handling an urn: Death of a friend. An urn full of ashes: Inheritance. Others moving an urn: Will ahieve distinction. An empty urn: Death among neighbours. A broken urn: Unhappiness. Ashes of a relative being put in an urn: Financial-gains.

V

VACATION:

Making plans for a vacation: Will have many happy days. Going on a vacation: Will have a wonderful time. Going on a vacation with a loved one: Will be persecuted. Returning from a vacation: Will enjoy prosperity. Others going on a vacation: Will enjoy a considerable fortune.

VALENTINE:

Of a Valentine Day: Excitement and joy, Sending valentines: Will lose an opportunity to make money. Receiving a valentine: Will take advantage of available opportunities. A sweetheart receiving a valentine: Victory over enemies. A sweetheart sending a valentine: Contradiction. Married people exchanging valentines: Will receive unexpected invitation. Children sending valentine to parents: Inheritance within a year.

VAN:

Of a van: Honour. An open van: Do not act impulsively. A covered van: Plans for a trip will not be realized. Getting out of a van: Loss of employment. Other people riding in a van: Good things come to one with patience.

VEGETABLES:

Of vegetables: Hard work with small rewards. Picking vegetables: Money worries will be greatly lessened by economy. Others picking vegetables: Quarrels. Vegetables that are still in the ground: Will suffer many afflictions. Eating vegetables: Losses in business. Green vegetables: Continue to preserve and retain high hopes. Smelling doors of vegetables cooking: Will discover unpleasant secrets.

VEIL:

Of a veil: Mystery and modesty. Having a veil: You are disguising something. Opening a veil or folding it: Favourable circumstances. Wearing a veil: You are secretive in your actions. Losing a veil: Will lose your lover. A bridal veil: Good prospects for great happiness. A woman wearing a veil: Beware of false advice. Arranging a veil on your head: Will be deceived. The veil over a dead person: Will assist at a wedding.

VICTORY:

Of victory: Unhappiness. Gaining victory over someone: Riches and honour. A military victory: People are lay going at you. A politicial victory: Increase in taxes. Being a member of a victorious team: Don't take sides in others' quarrels.

VIOLENCE:

Violence being done to others: Will have parties with friends. Showing violence yourself: Better days ahead. Being attacked with violence: Joy. Mate showing violence: Indifelity.

VOTE:

Of voting: You must be atpeace with yourself to attain desires. Casting a ballot: Will be favoured by good luck. Voting for someone you know: Hopes will be fulfilled. Voting for political offices: Will receive good news. Voting for people to hold position in church: Virtue and blessings of God.

VOYAGE:

Being on a voyage: Will receive an inheritance. Taking a voyage: Will receive a message soon from faraway. Taking a voyage alone: Good times are in view in the future. Taking a voyage to foreign countries with family: Fortune. Taking a voyage and being in a foreign country: Reflect well upon actions. Taking a voyage with sweetheart: Gossip.

W

WAGES:

Receiving wages: Danger of small thefts. Preparing the payroll: Bad temper and disappointment. Paying wages: Will loss money received from a legacy. Paying weekly wages: A better future awaits. Paying wages to labourers: Will have to work hard all during life. Paying wages to white-collar workers: A beautiful woman will be married. Receiving own wages: Loss. Being refused payment of wages: Will have a lawsuit. Not receiving wages for work performed: Bankruptcy.

WAIT:

Of waiting for someone to arrive: A false friends is nearby. Waiting in readiness for action: A friend is trying to help you reccently. Waiting on people: Advancement within own position. Waiting for arrival of someone delayed: Insurmountable obstacles ahead. Waiting for a loved one to arrive: Good times are coming.

WAR:

Of war: Troubles and danger. Making war with someone: Persecution. Watching a war: Misfortune. Being in a war: Danger of illness. Documents of war: Joy. Winning a war: Happiness. Lossing a war: Loss of unimportant papers.

WASH:

Of washing: A service will be rendered by an unknown person. Washing in clear water: Will enjoy many pleasures in life. Washing hands in cold water: Conentment. Washing hands in hot water: Success. Washing feet. Anxiety. Washing hair or beard: Sorrow. Washing body: Beware of immoral conduct. Washing food: Happy life. Washing linen: Difficulties ahead. Washing a dishes: Friends will visit at your home.

WATER FALL:

Of a waterfall: Will be invited to a place of amusement. A clear waterfall: Happiness. Viewing a waterfall with others: You are being watched and gossiped about. Taking water from a water-fall: Troubles will be very few.

WATERMELON:

Of a watermelon: Good success. Eating watermelon: Vain hopes. Buying watremelon: Fortune. Growing watermelon: Will receive a gift from an unknown person. Giving children watermelon to eat: Happiness. Sick people dreaming of eating watermelon: Will soon recover.

WEAK:

Being weak: Rapid success of own hopes. Mate being weak: Realization of high ambitions. Children being weak: Financial gains. Friends being weak: Will have good earnings.

WEALTH:

Unmarried people dreaming of wealth: Will marry poor people. Rich people dreaming of wealth: Illness. Poor people dreaming of wealth. Will have good earnings. Being wealthy: Unhappiness in love affairs. Receiving a wealthy inheritance:

Family quarrels. Having wealthy relatives: Important and very beneficial events to come. Having a wealthy mate: Luck and prosperity. Having wealthy friends: They will endeavor to destroy you.

WEATHER:

Of beautiful weather: Security in everything. Terrible weather: Will have unpleasant news. Windy weather: Big friendship. Stormy weather: Enemies are seeking your ruin. Rainy weather: You will receive a letter that will cause sadness.

WEDDING:

Of a wedding: Happy days are ahead. Being at a wedding: Big advantages will come to you. A relative's wedding: Expect trouble in the family circle. Husband or wife attending a wedding: Profit. Attending a sister's wedding: Big danger. Attending a brother's wedding: Will make money. Attending the wedding of a virgin: Honour. Attending the wedding of a son: Approaching money. Attending the wedding of a daughter: Wealth. Attending the wedding of a widow: Will make abundant money.

WEDDING RING:

Of a wedding ring: Dignity and fortune. Losing a wedding ring: Vexation. Receiving a wedding ring: Domestic happiness. A wedding ring being covered with diamonds: Good health.

WHITE:

Of the color white: Success in undertakings. Buying white linen: Money will come easily during life. Various white-colored materials: Big joy. Buying white clothes:

Happiness in love.

WIDOW:

Of a widow: Will soon receive happy news. A woman dreaming of being a widow: Joy and health. A widow marrying: You have reached the last resort. A widow marrying a rich old man: Happiness is assured. A widow marrying a young man: Misfortune in love affairs. A rich widow marrying a poor man: Insurmountable obstacles are ahead. A widow marrying a distant relative: Change of surroundings.

WIFE:

Of your own wife: Must control your passions. Taking a wife: Accomplishment of desires. Being called by your wife: Will be tormented. Arguing with your wife: Will have a quarrel lasting several days. Wife being beautifully dressed: Warning of trouble. Own wife undressing: You must mend your ways in life. Own wife being naked: She is cheating on you. Wife being in a bathtub: Misfortune in love affairs. Wife lying in the sun at the beach: Will avoid a present peril. Wife swimming at a pool: A rival will steel her affections. Wife being married to another: Change of affairs or separation. A wife dreaming of being married to another man: Sudden separation or death of husband.

WIRELESS:

Of wireless: Will receive unexpected good news concerning money. Using a wireless machine: Will have many friends. Operating a wireless machine: Prompt engagement. Sending messages by wireless: Family afflictions. Receiving messages by wireless: You are very cruel. A wireless machinke being broken: You have many enemies. Being at an office of wireless machines: Money will come easily in life. A wireless machine being abroad a ship: Beware of danger.

WOOL:

Of wool: Success at home and in business. The wool of a sheep: You are prone to using flattery too much. The wool of a lamb: You are a very kind and easygoing person. Selling wool: will enjoy a comfortable life. Buying wool: Prosperity and success. Making material from raw wool: Will live a long life. Selling clothes made of wool: Great unhappiness. Buying wool clothes: Loss of a friend.

WORSHIP:

Of worshiping: Great honours and riches. Worshiping in church: Desires will be accomplished. Worshiping the Lord: Great joy. Worshiping at home: Unhappiness. Family worshiping: Joy. Teaching children to worship: Persecution.

WRESTLE:

Of wrestling: Disputes. Wrestling with debtors: Will receive assistance. Wrestling with very strong people: Infirmity and sickness. Wrestling with professionals: Enemies will be punished. Wrestling with crazy people: Death. Wrestling with prisoners: Liberation. Wrestling with friends: Will be elevated to a better position. Wrestling with children: Unexpected fortune. Wrestling with snakes: Severe punishment of enemies. Wrestling with wild beasts: Hard work ahead. Others wrestling with crazy people: Loss of a lawsuit.

WRITE:

Writing on paper: Will be falsely accused of something. Writing letters: Someone is stealing from you. Of writing:

Foretells a serious error which will threaten your peace. Writing in capital letters: Joy. Writing a report: Will be accused of slander. Writing memoirs: Dishonour. Writing an agenda: Infirmity. Writing love letter to mate: Happiness and unity. Writing a letter to relatives: Profit. Writing a letter to children: Must put out money. Writing a business letter: Will collect money. Writing a reminder letter of payment due: Bad success.

X

X RAY:

Of an X-ray machine: Worry will be smoothed away. Having own X-ray taken: Doomed for disappointment. Having a favourable X-ray report: Important and very beneficial event to come. X-ray reports of others: Family quarrels. Operating an X-ray machine: Will have good earnings.

Y

YACHT:

Of a yacht: Good luck. A yacht under full sail: Pleasant visit in a nice place. A yacht under full engine speed: Big joy. A yacht sailing on a smooth sea: Prosperily. Being on a yacht: Realization of your own ambitions. A yacht sailing on rough sea: Disappointments. A stranded yacht: Business ventures will cause you distress.

YANKEE:

Of a yankee: You will fulfill your duty with honour. Fighting with people of same nationality: Joy. Fighting between two states: Honour. The North fighting the South: Will receive good news.

YEAR:

Of a year: Will be feeble from age. Leap year: Will make small profits. A year ending in even numbers: Will have very little money. A year ending in odd numbers: Will inherit plenty of money.

YELLOW:

Of the color yellow: Important changes in your affairs.

YIELD:

Of yielding: Don't believe flattering talk. Yielding to

persuasive words: A false friend is nearby. Lovers yielding to persuasive stories: Danger in love affairs. Others yielding to your persuasive words: You have too much pride.

YOUNG:

An aged person dreaming of being young: Will receive happy news. An aged woman dreaming of being young: Will have a devoted husband. Of becoming young again: Important and very beneficial events to come. Being young: A change for the better will not last long.

Z

ZEBRA:

Of a zebra: Will do extensive travel abroad. A zebra at a zoo: Friendship is badly placed. A mother zebra with her young: Disagreements with friends. A zebra being attacked by wild animals: Your honour is in danger. A zebra being fed at a zoo: Ingratitude.

ZENITH:

Of that point of the heavens vertically above you: Happiness. An unmarried person dreaming of zenith: Good choice of husband or wife. A married person dreaming of zenith: Unusual wealth. Divorced people dreaming of zenith: Will marry a rich man or rich woman. A widower dreaming of zenith: Will never get married again. Widow dreaming of zenith: Will marry a younger man.

ZERO:

Of a zero: Will have a small unhappiness. Double zeros: Will be double-crossed by a friend. Three zeros: Will have great wealth. It being the zero hour: Success in all ventures.

ZIGZAG:

Of zigzag: Will go out of your mind. Walking zigzag: Business will endure bad consequences. Zigzagging with a horse: Will have changes in business. Zigzagging with a car: You will have many changeable mods. Children going zigzag: